I0488998

How To Draw Different Butterfly Tattoos

Complete Guide To Different **Butterfly** Tattoo Drawings

Butterfly Tattoo

By : Gala Publication

2

Published By :

Gala Publication
© Copyright 2015 – Gala Publication

ISBN-13: **978-1522707455**
ISBN-10: **152270745X**

Table of Contents

BUTTERFLIES
TATTOO

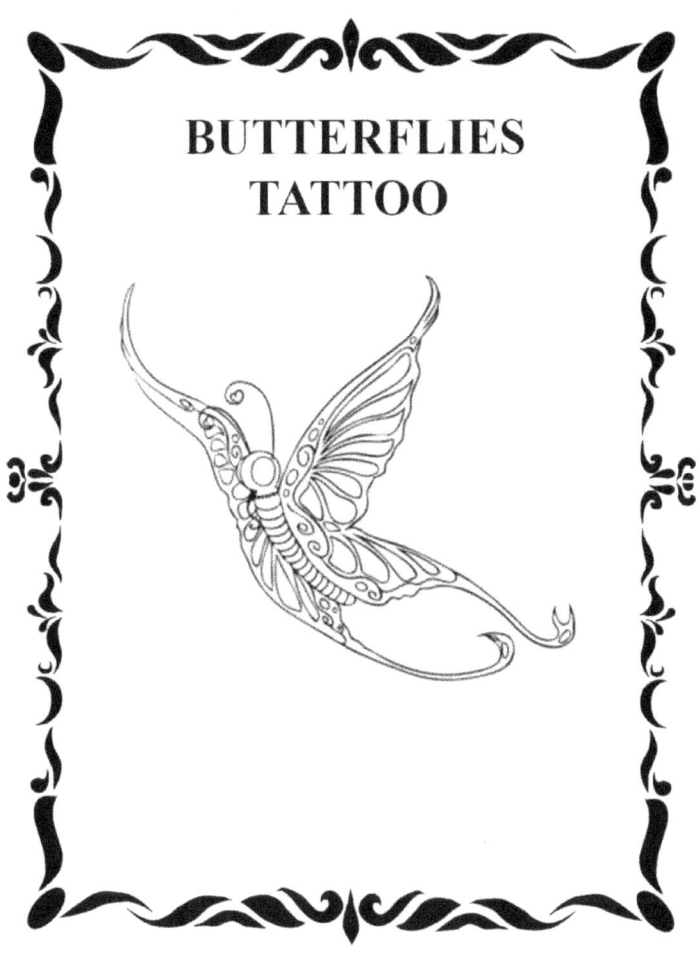

STEP 1

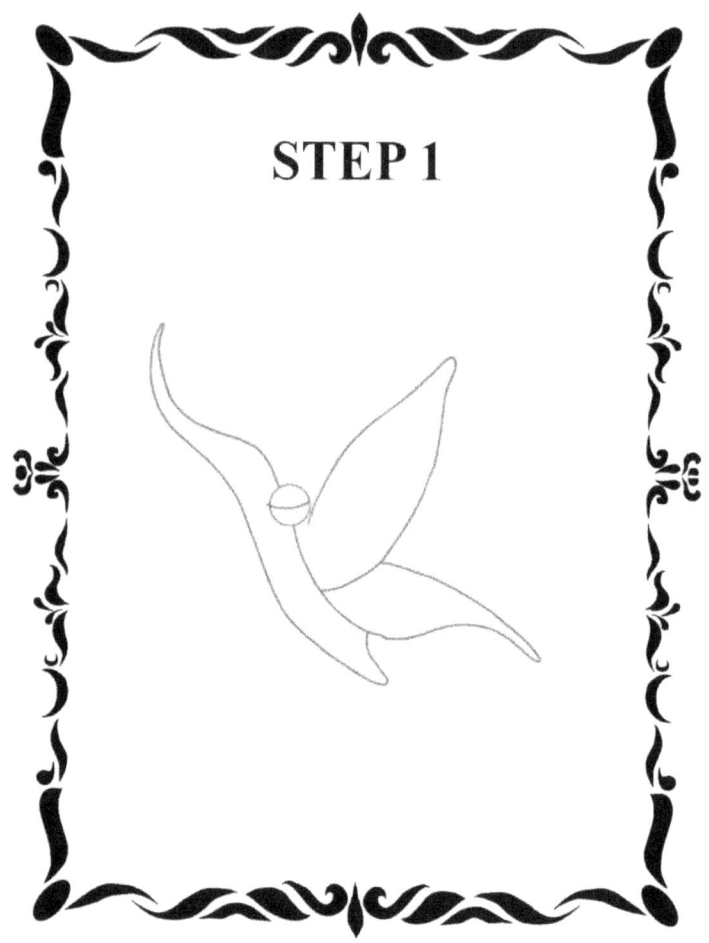

STEP 2

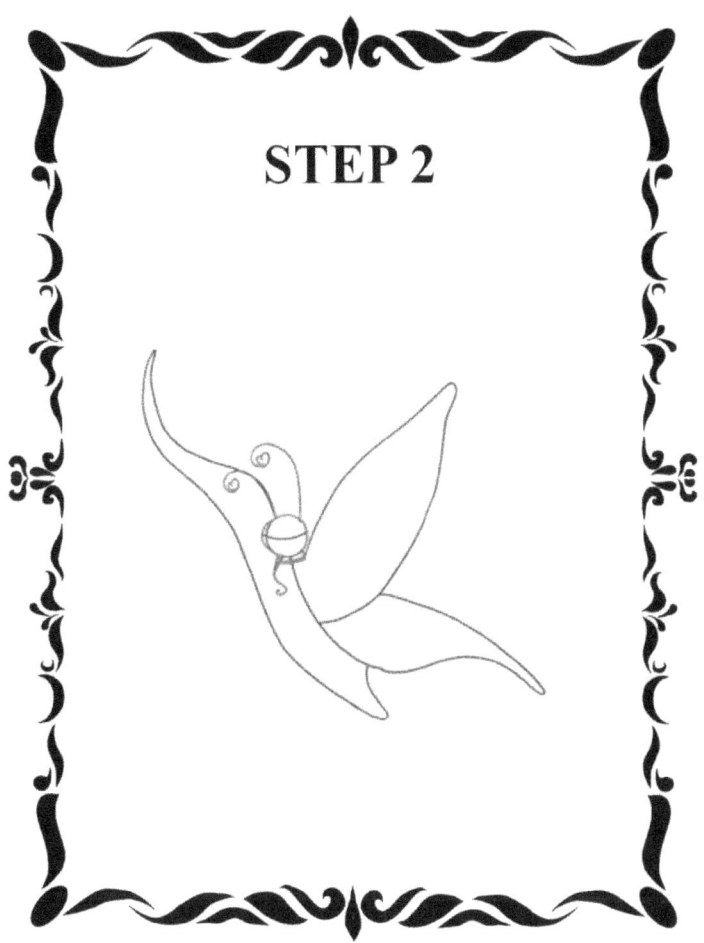

STEP 3

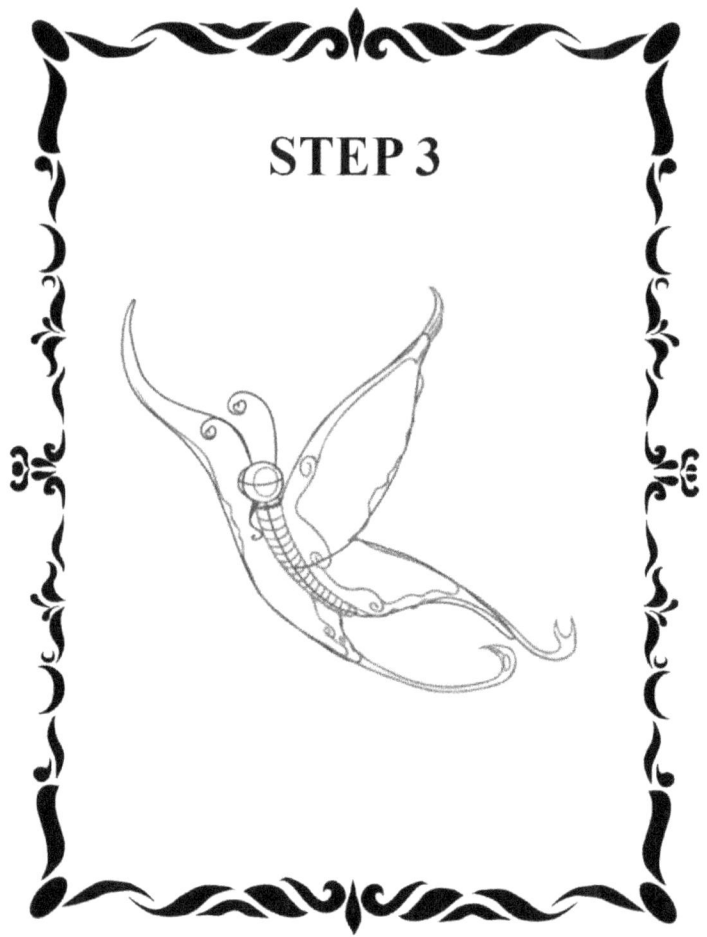

STEP 4

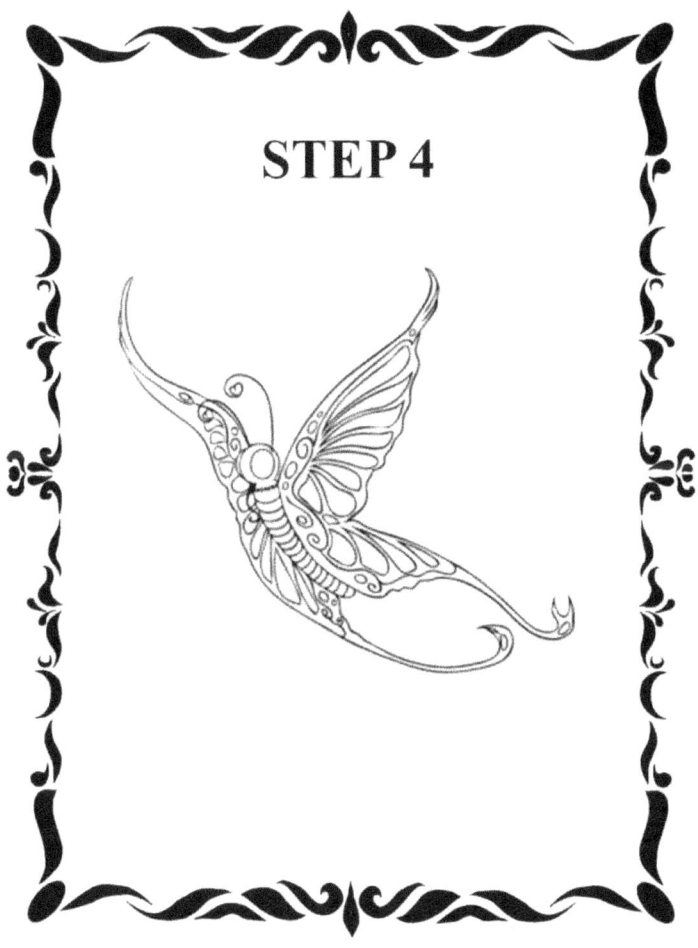

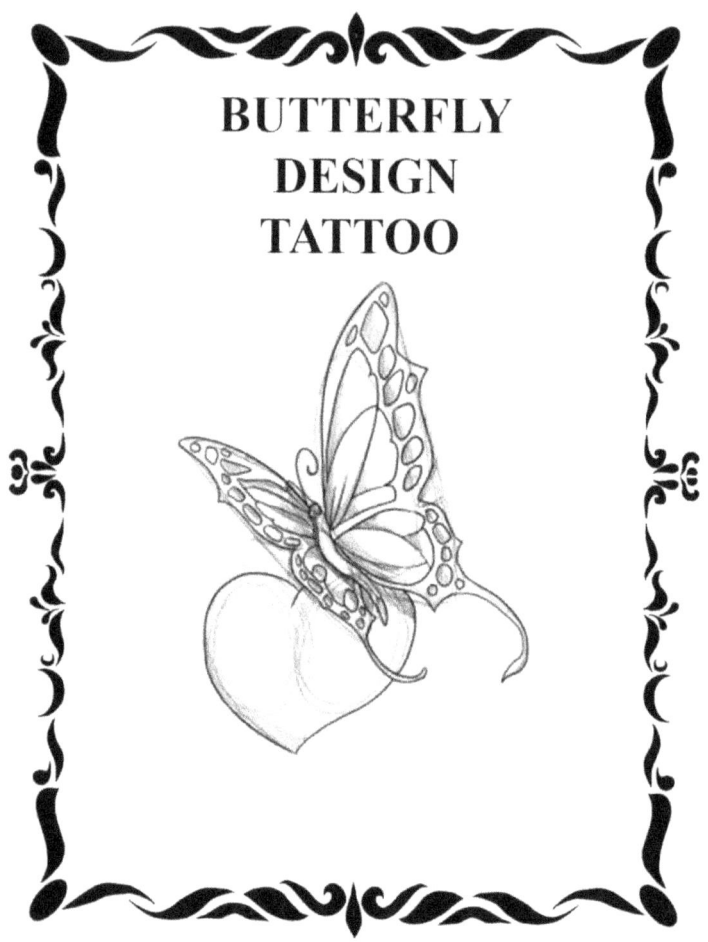

BUTTERFLY DESIGN TATTOO

STEP 1

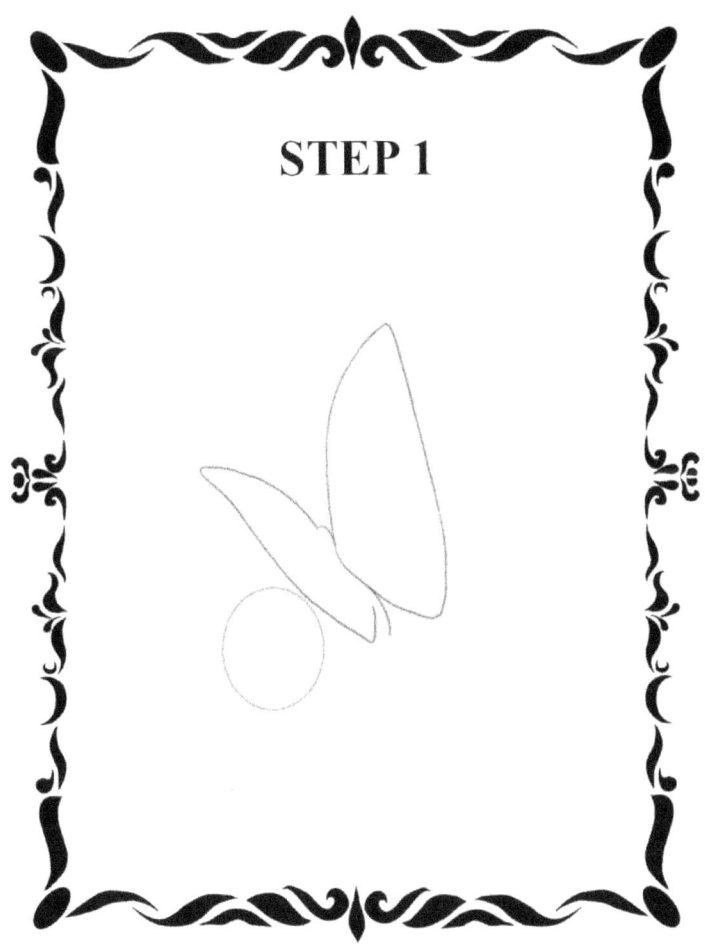

STEP 2

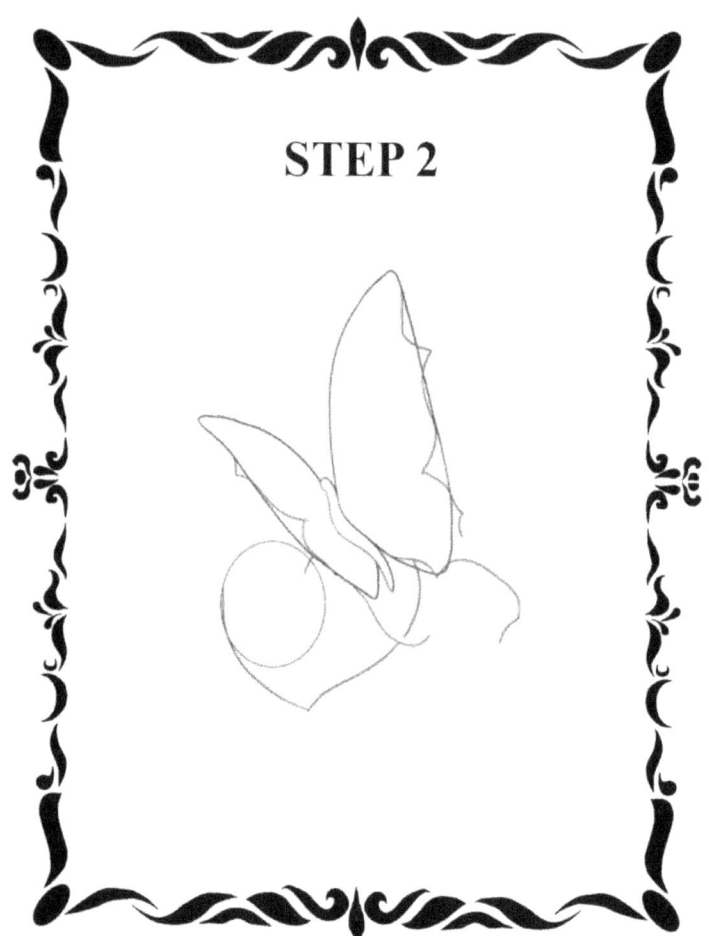

STEP 3

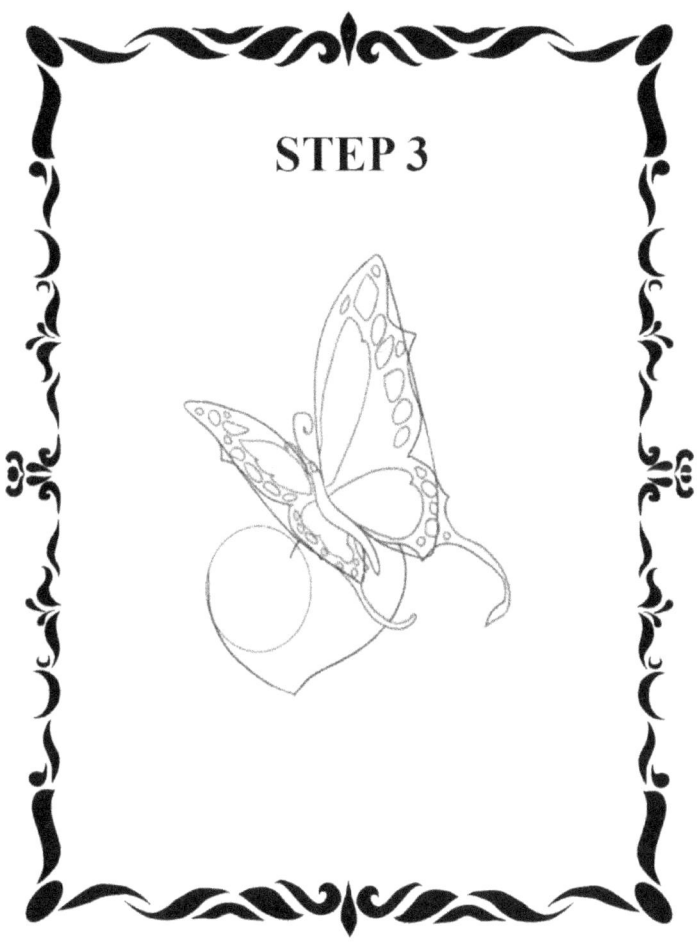

STEP 4

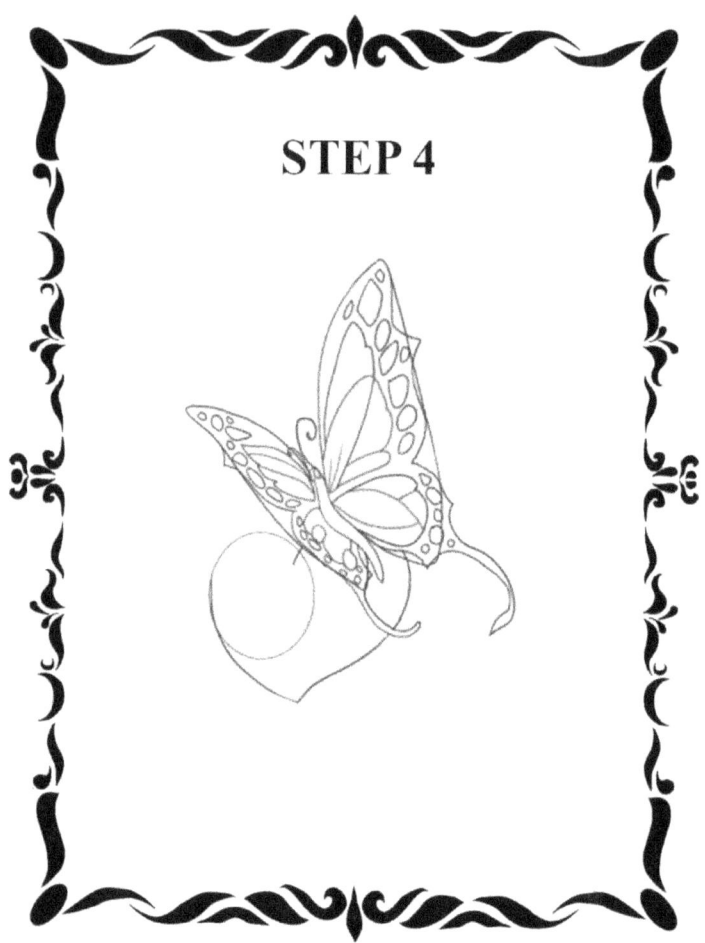

STEP 5

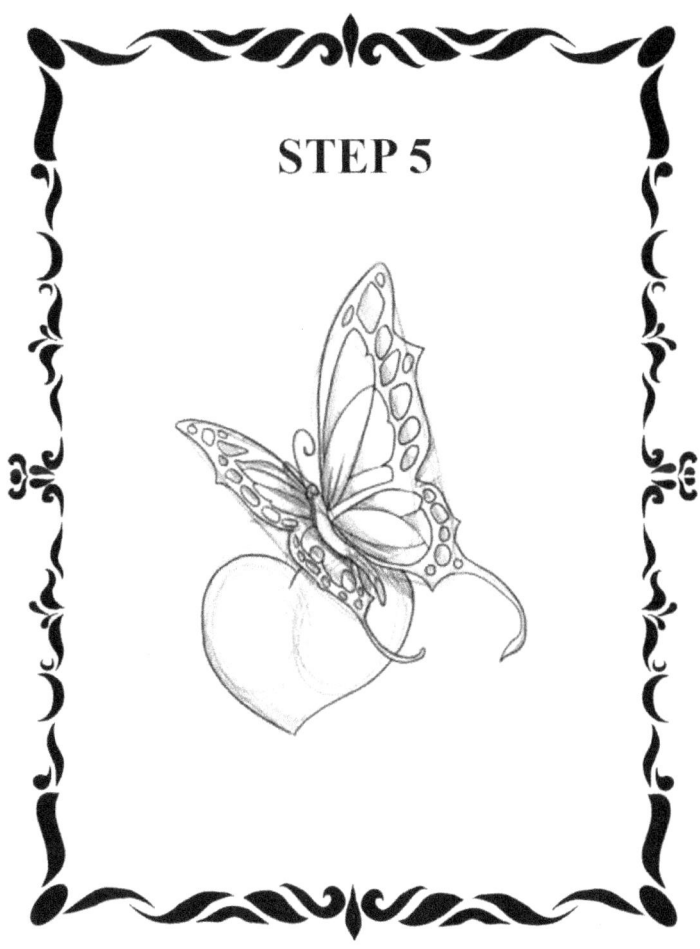

BUTTERFLY EYES TATTOO

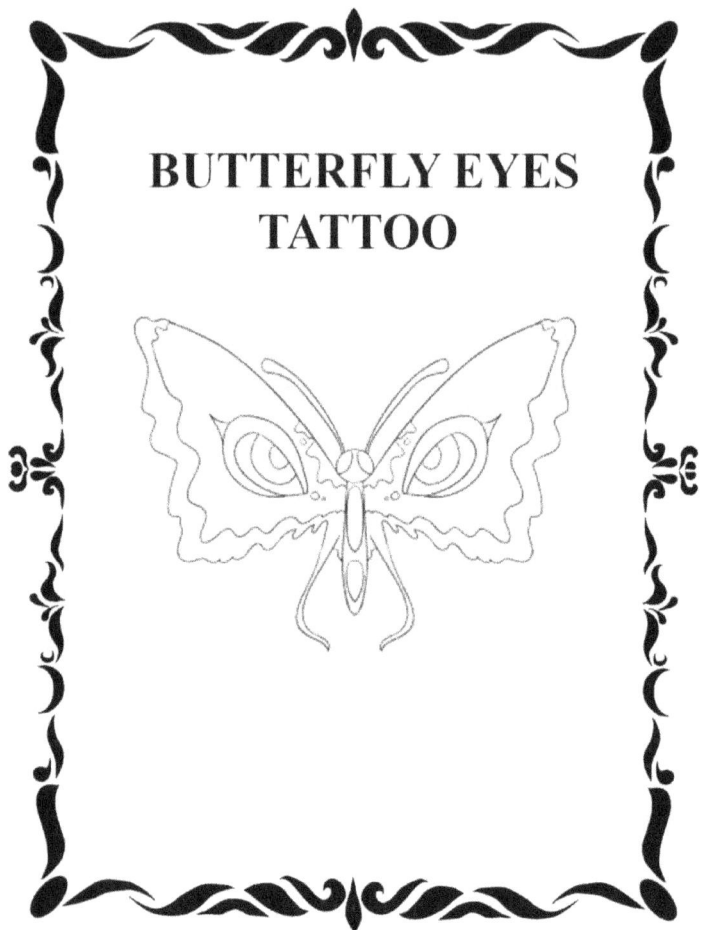

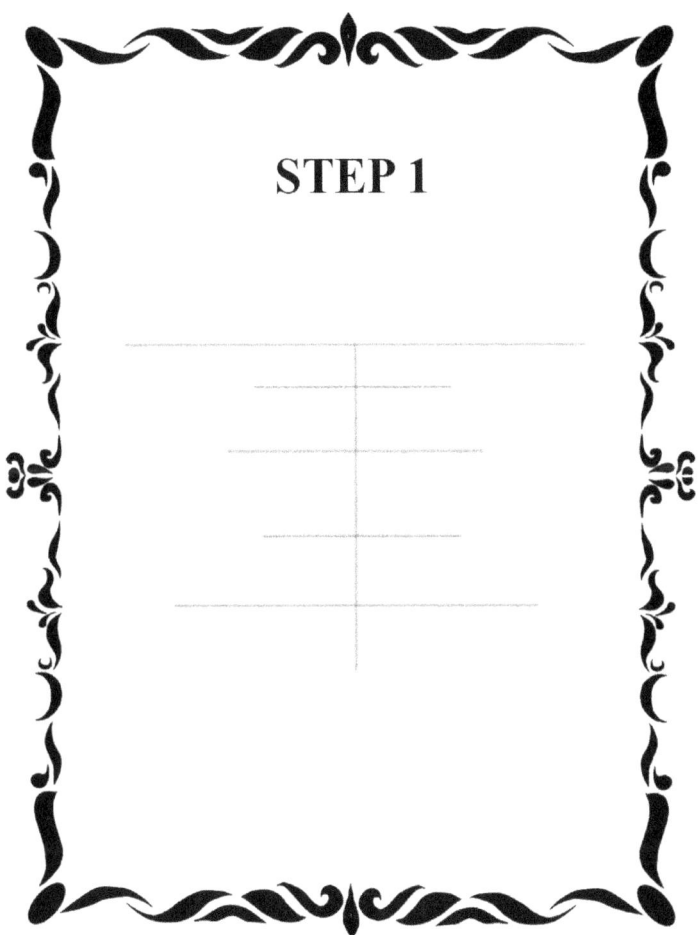

STEP 1

STEP 2

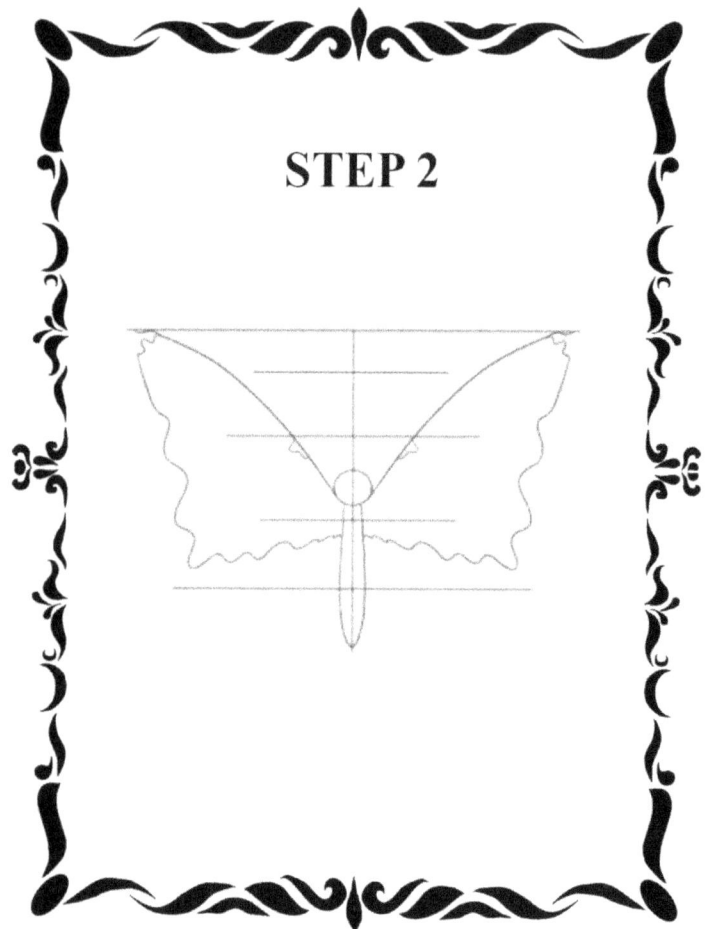

STEP 3

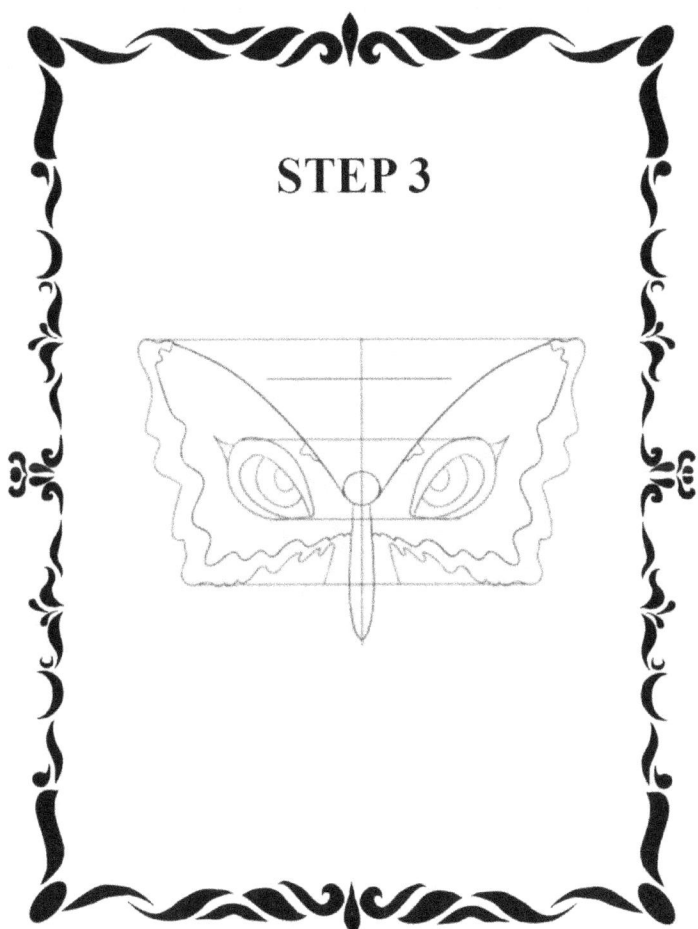

STEP 4

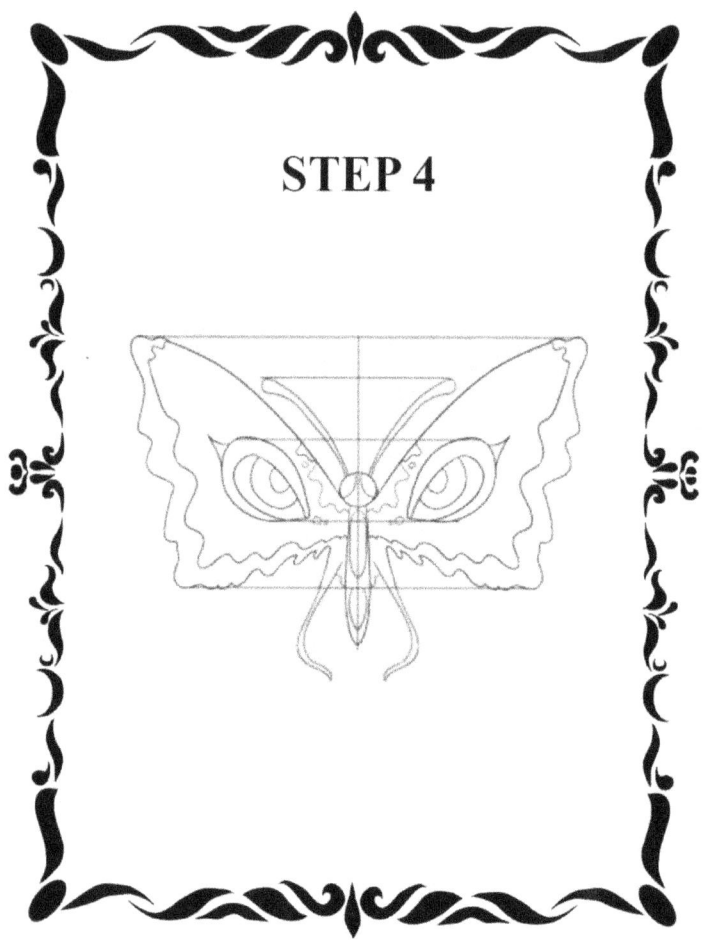

STEP 5

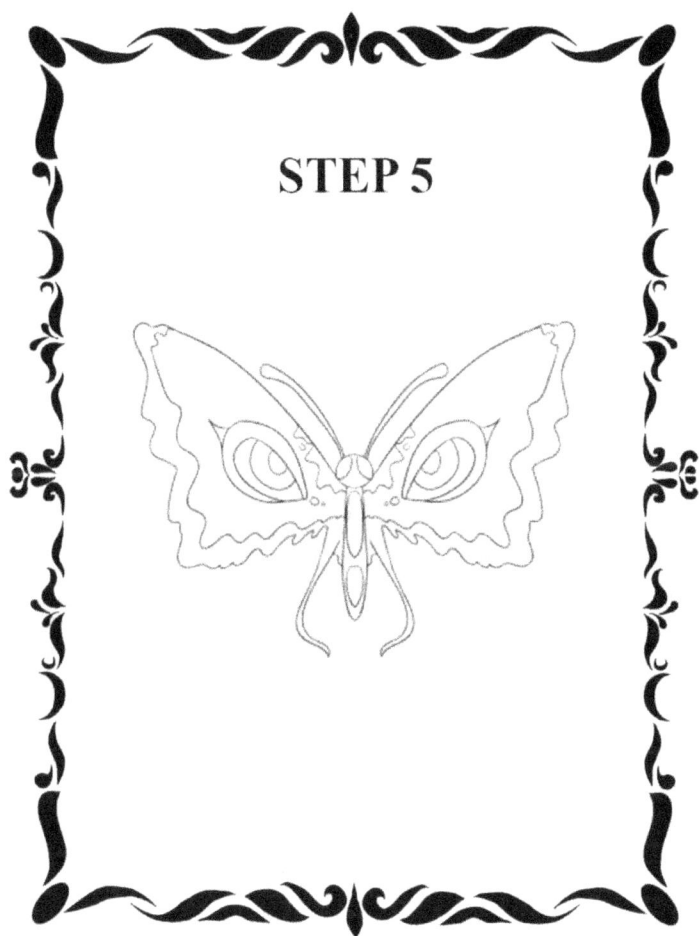

BUTTERFLY TATTOO

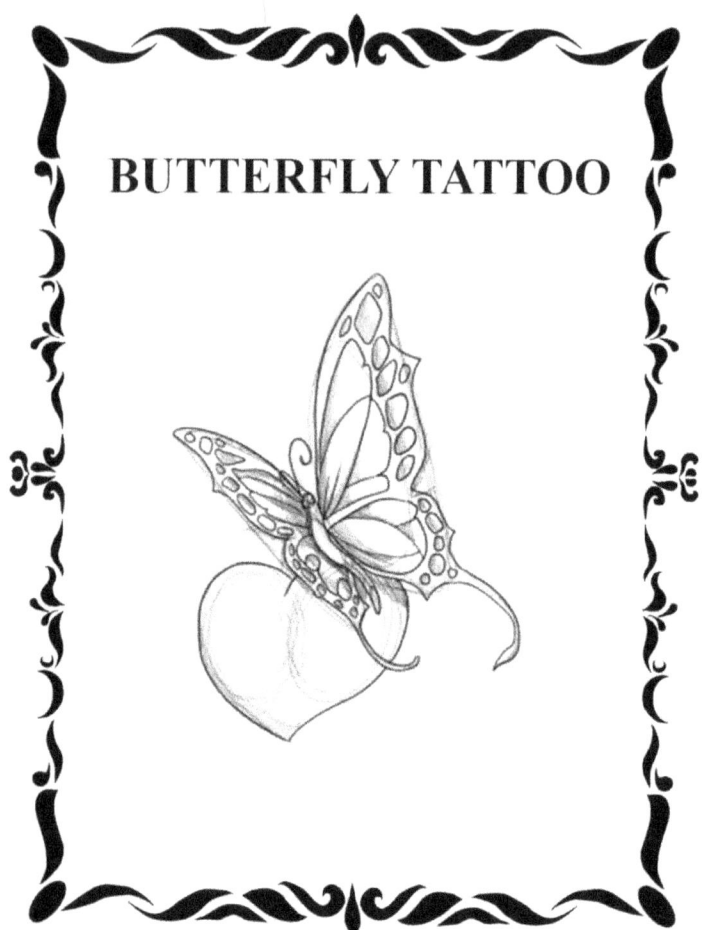

STEP 1

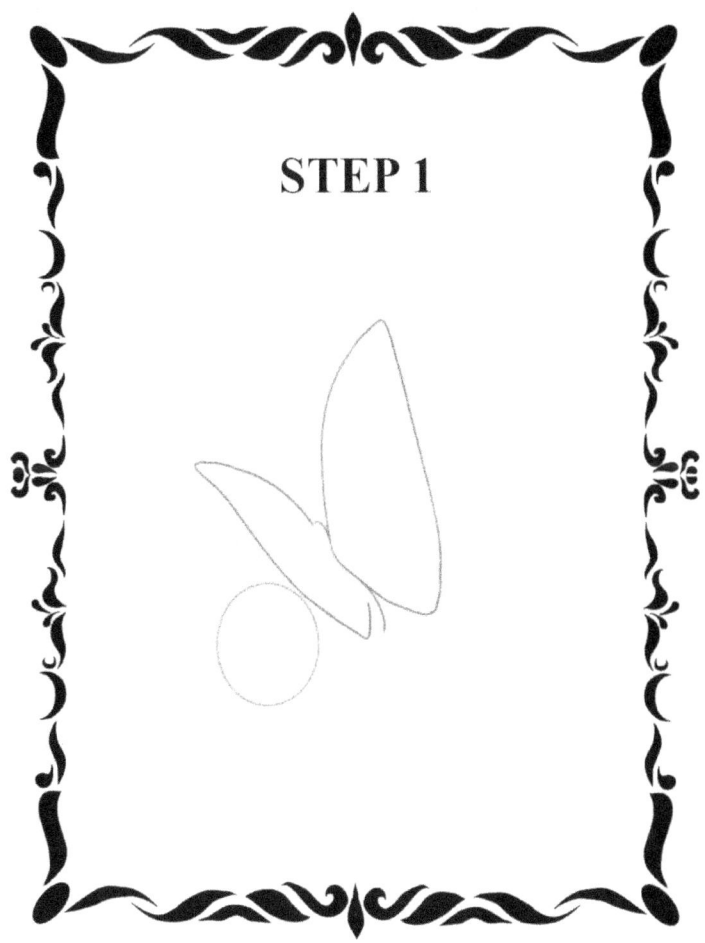

STEP 2

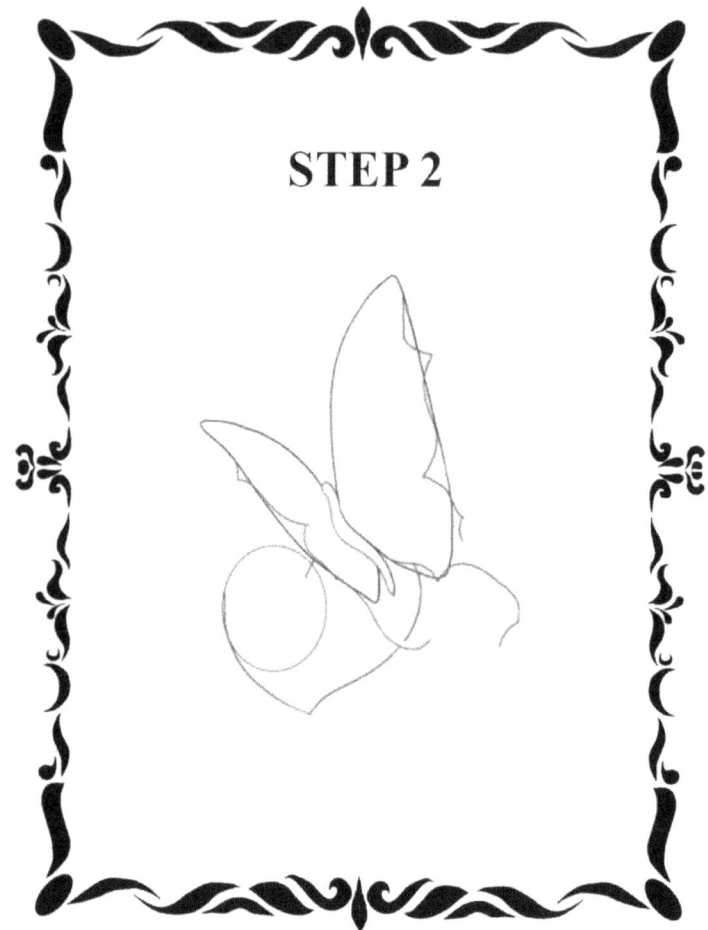

STEP 3

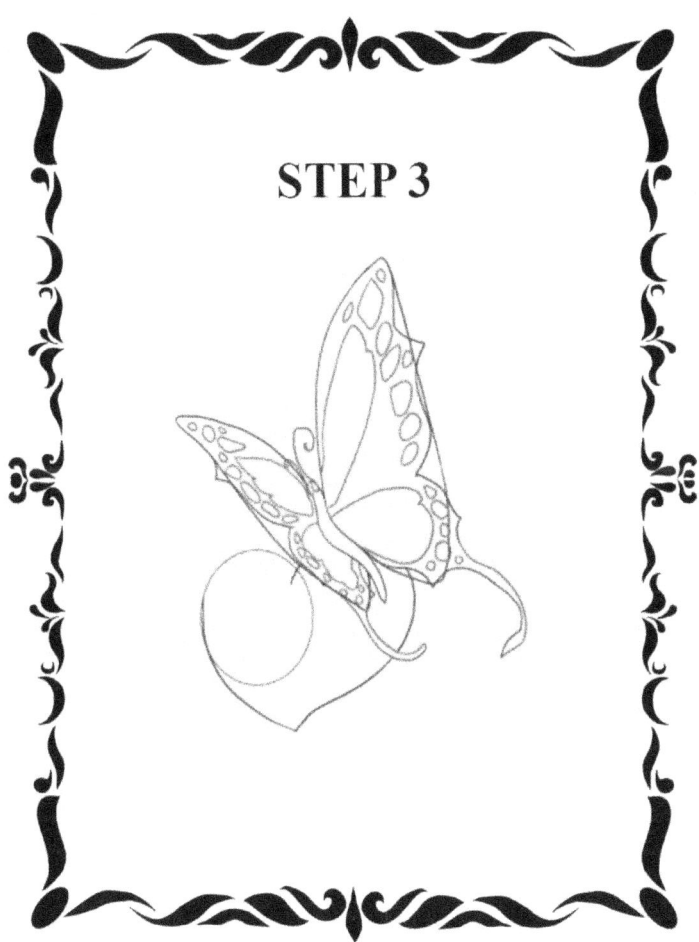

26

STEP 4

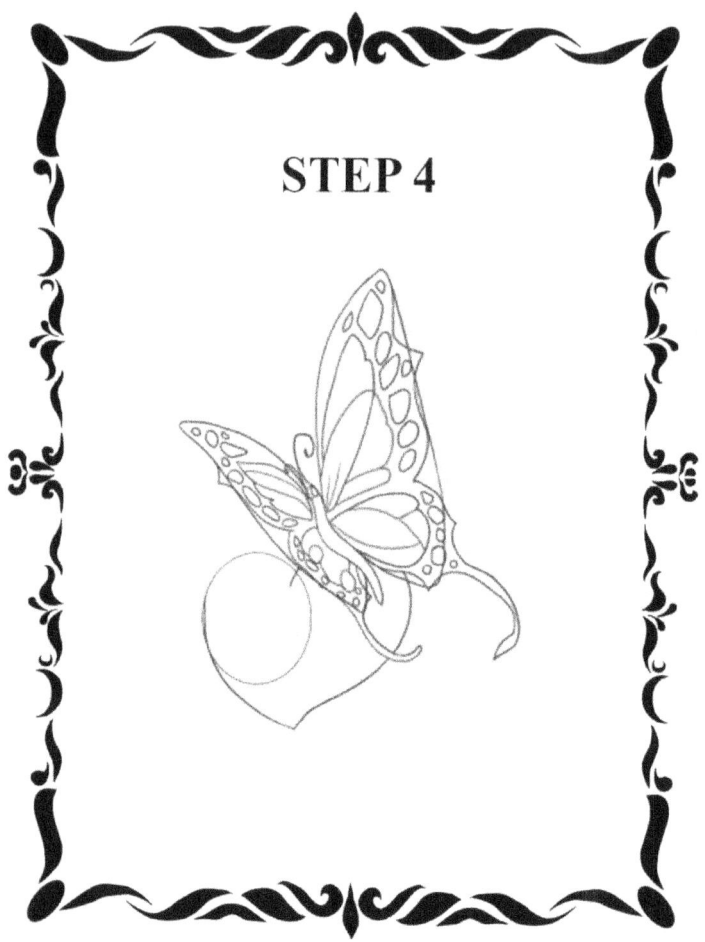

STEP 5

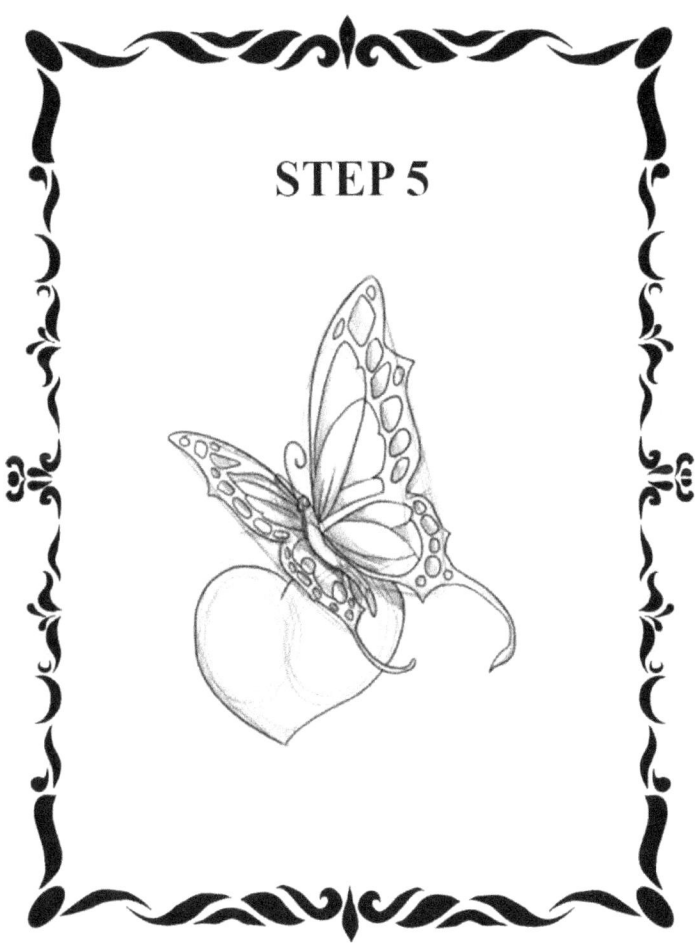

CARTOON BUTTERFLY

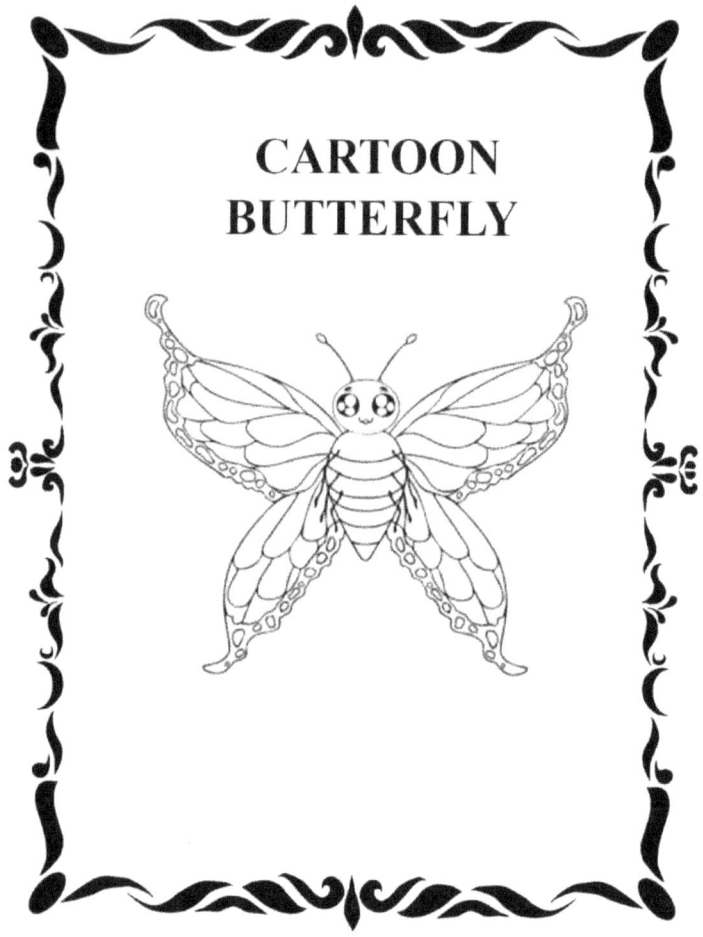

STEP 1

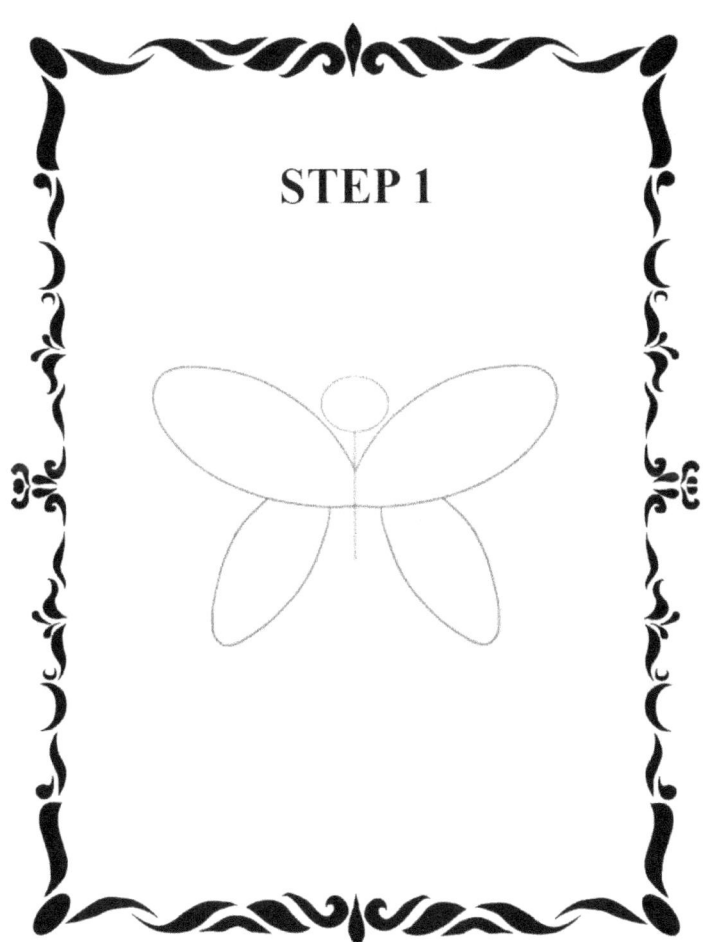

STEP 2

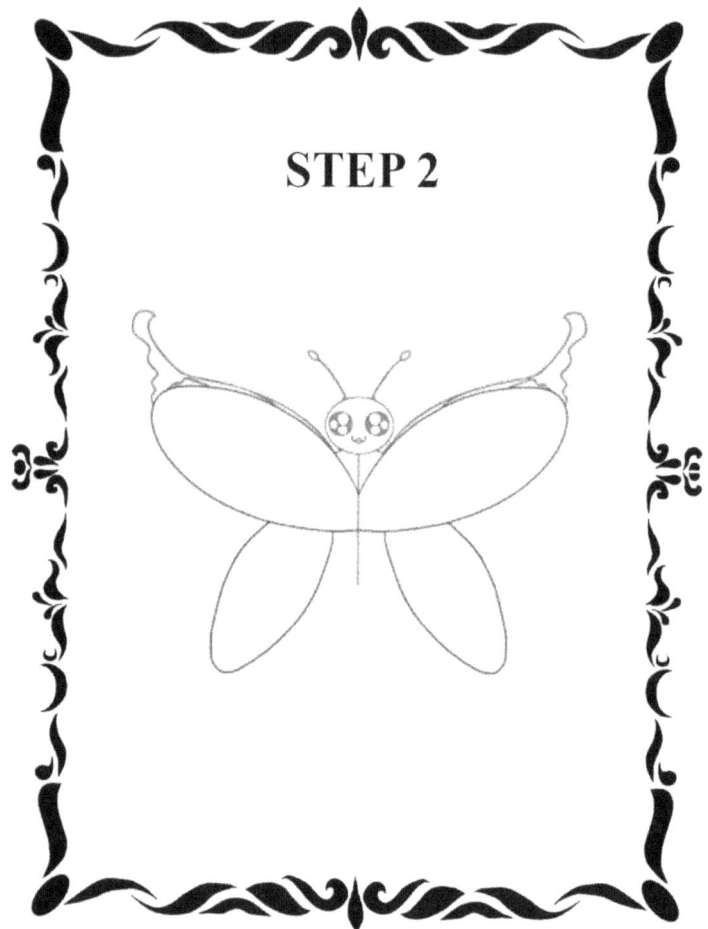

STEP 3

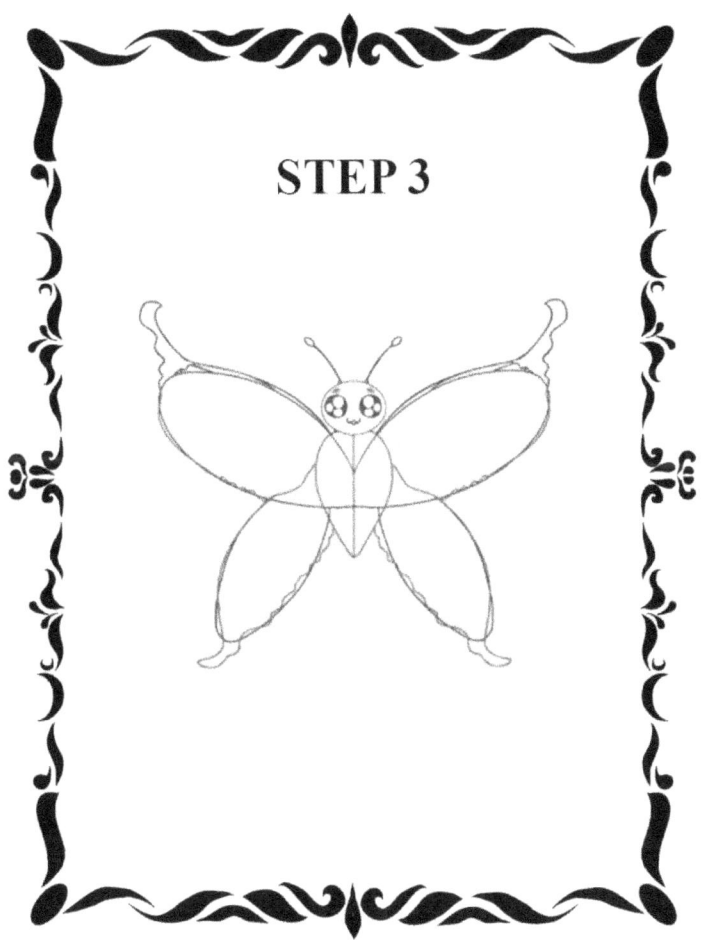

STEP 4

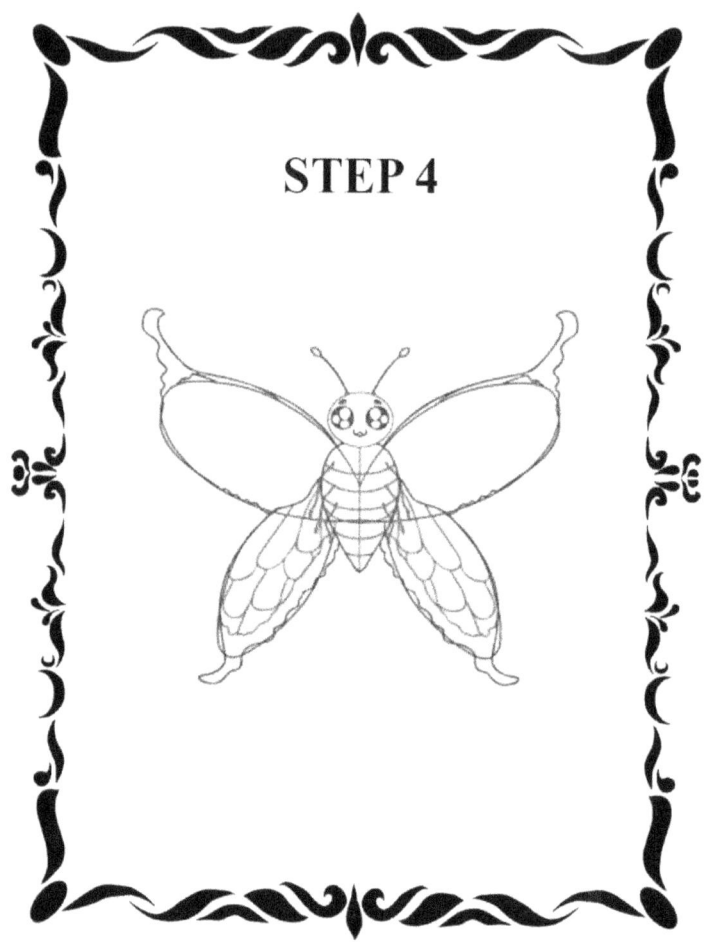

STEP 5

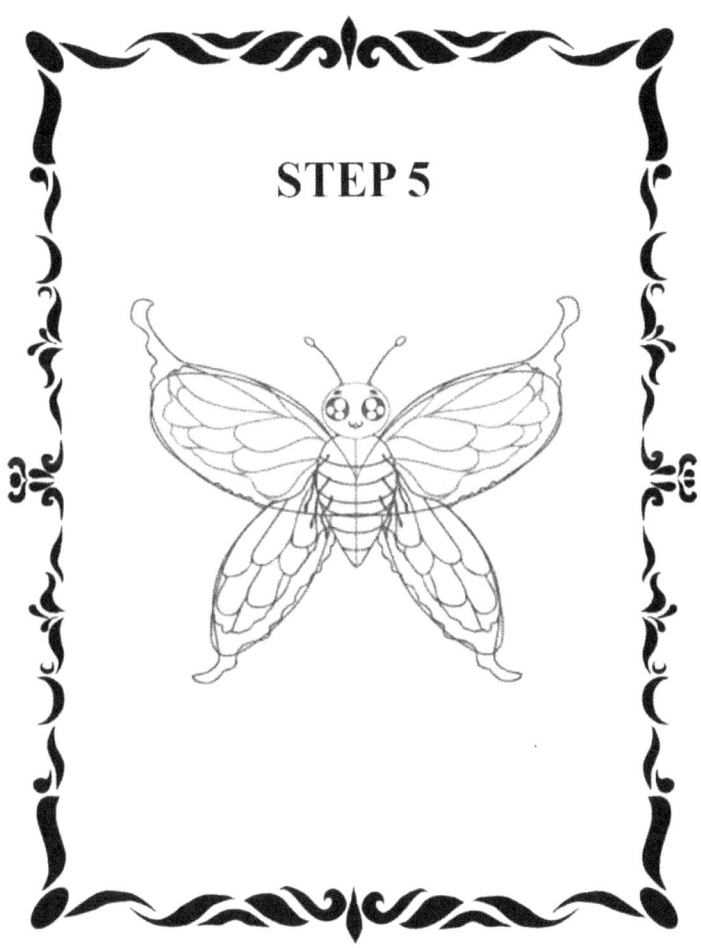

STEP 6

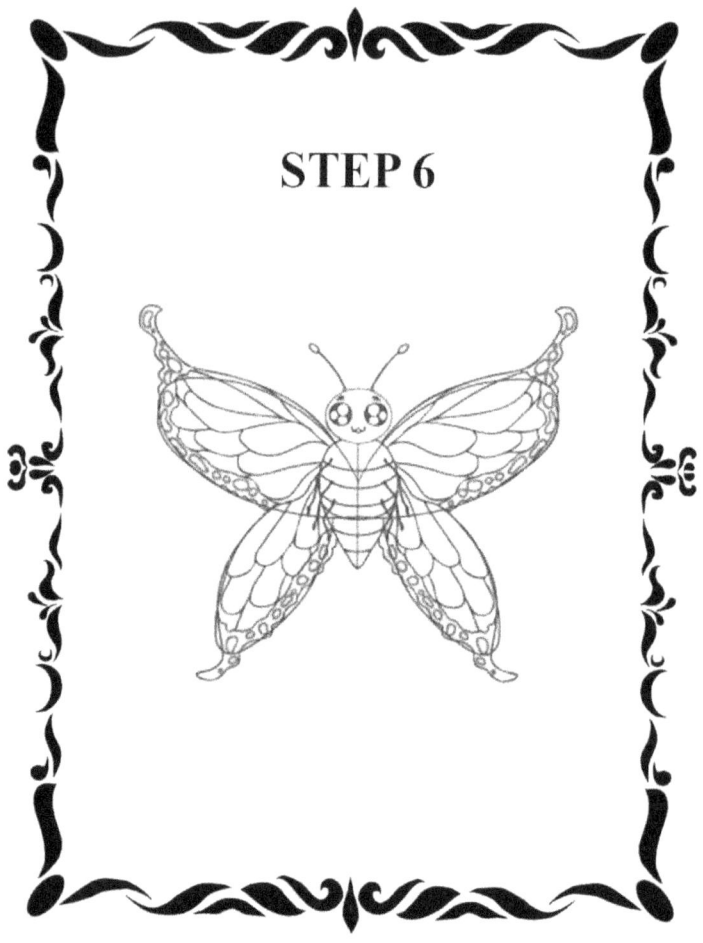

STEP 7

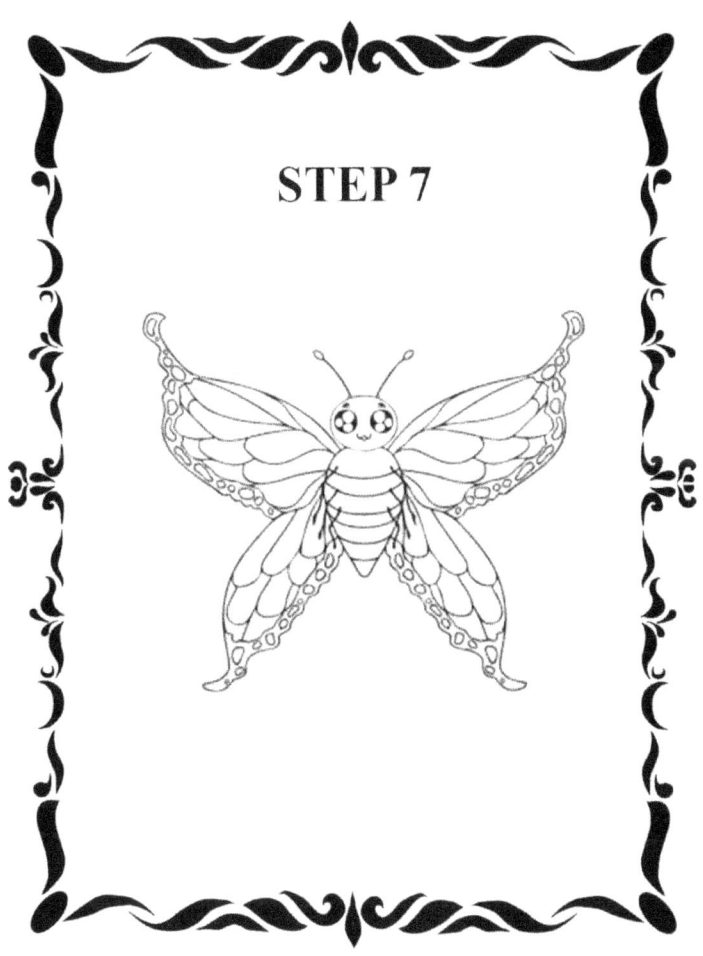

EASY
BUTTERFLY

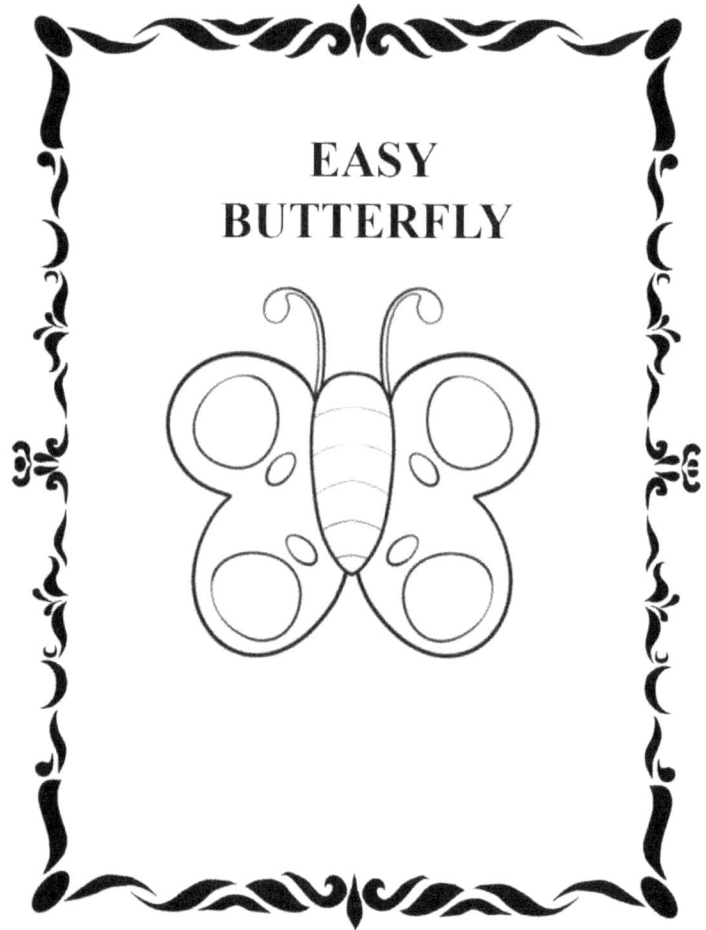

STEP 1

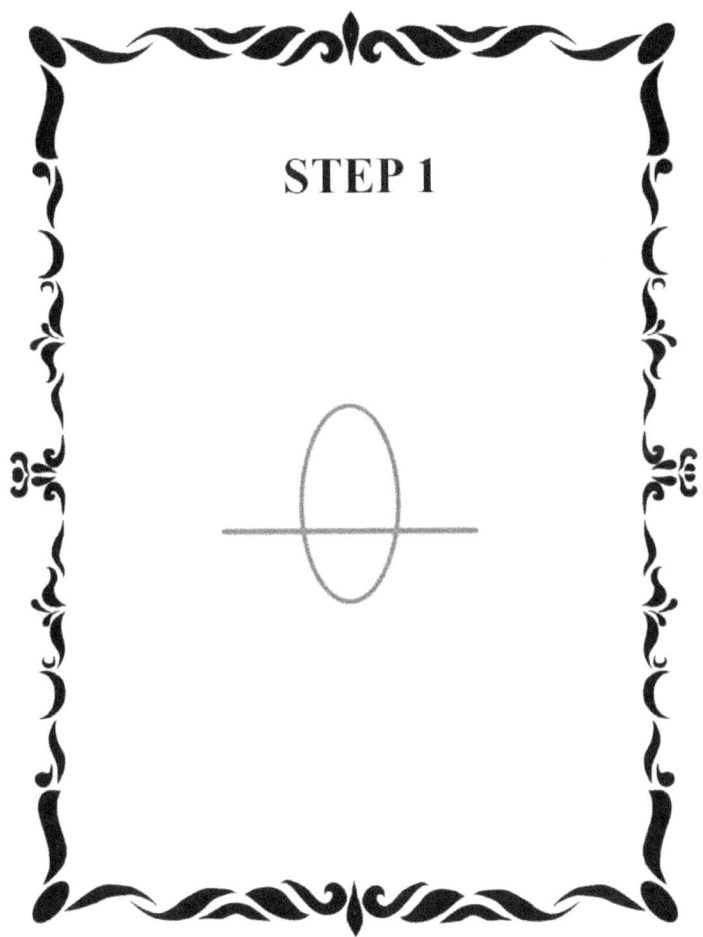

STEP 2

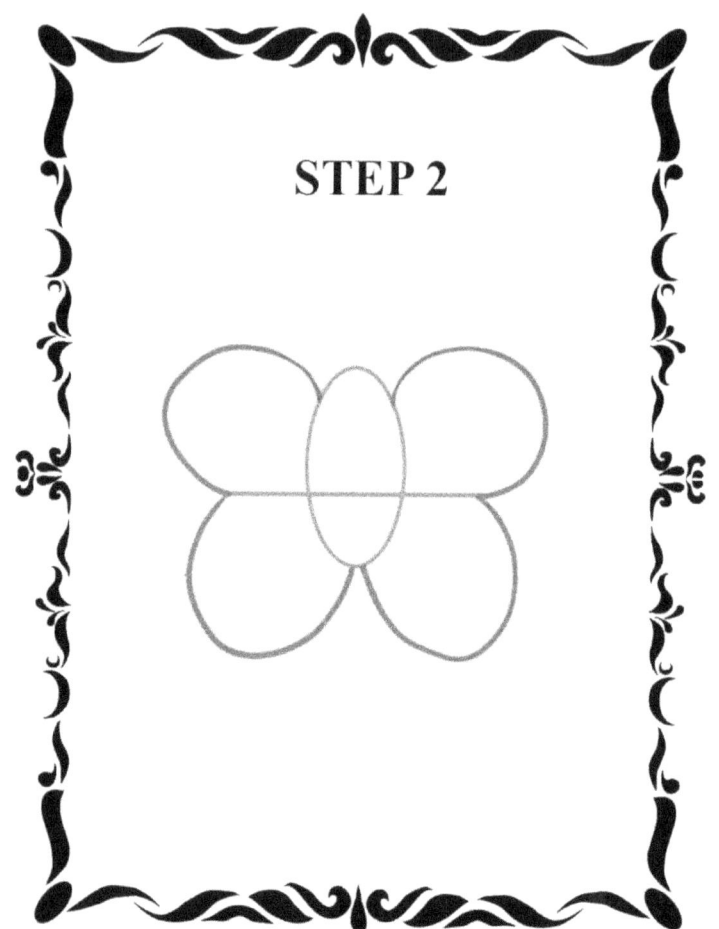

STEP 3

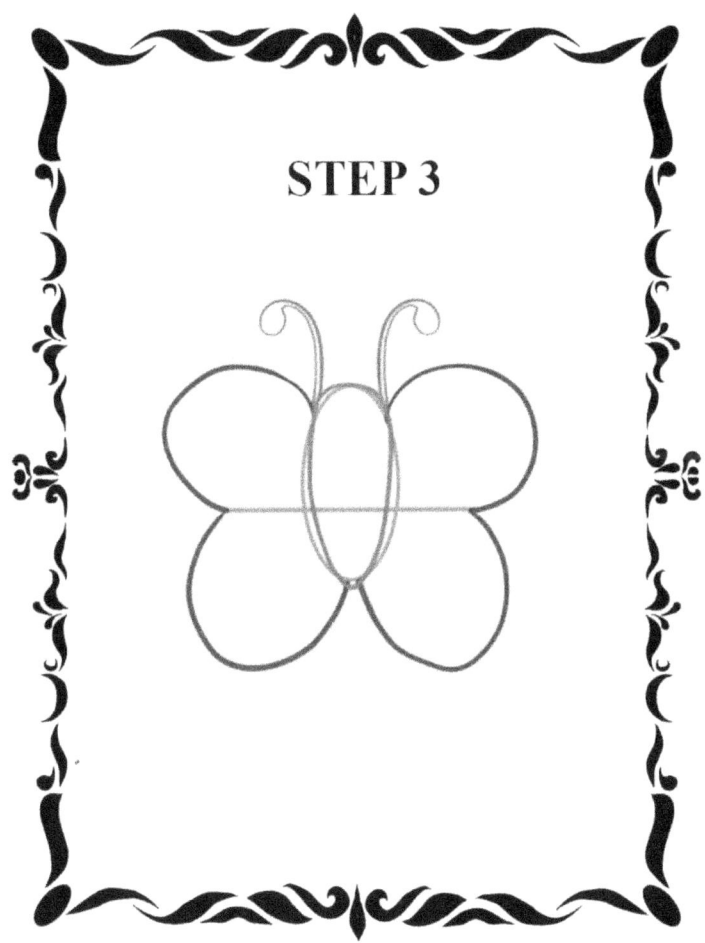

STEP 4

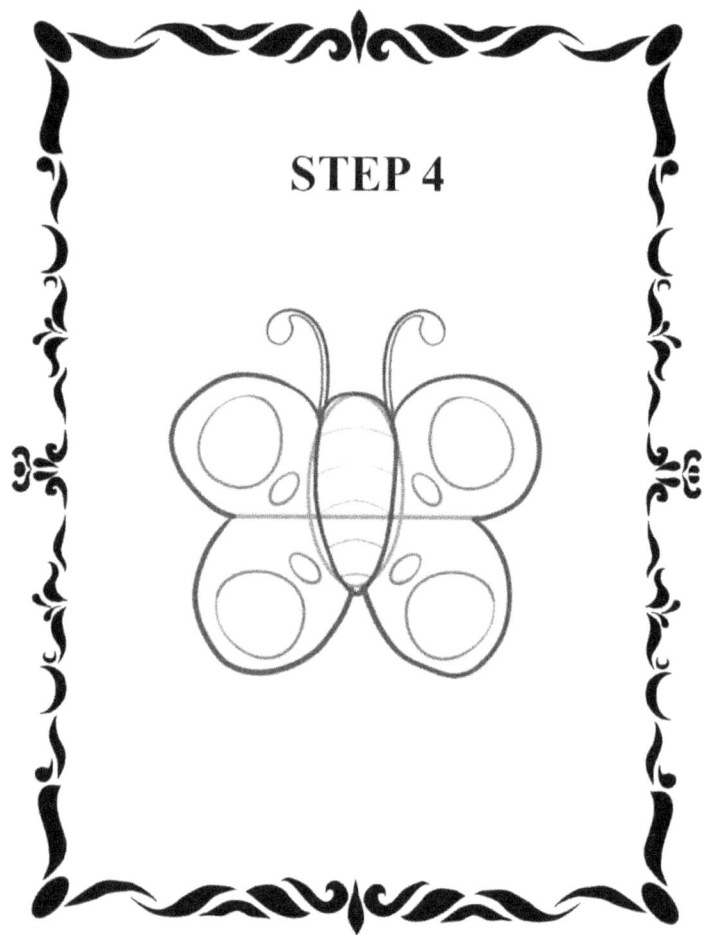

STEP 5

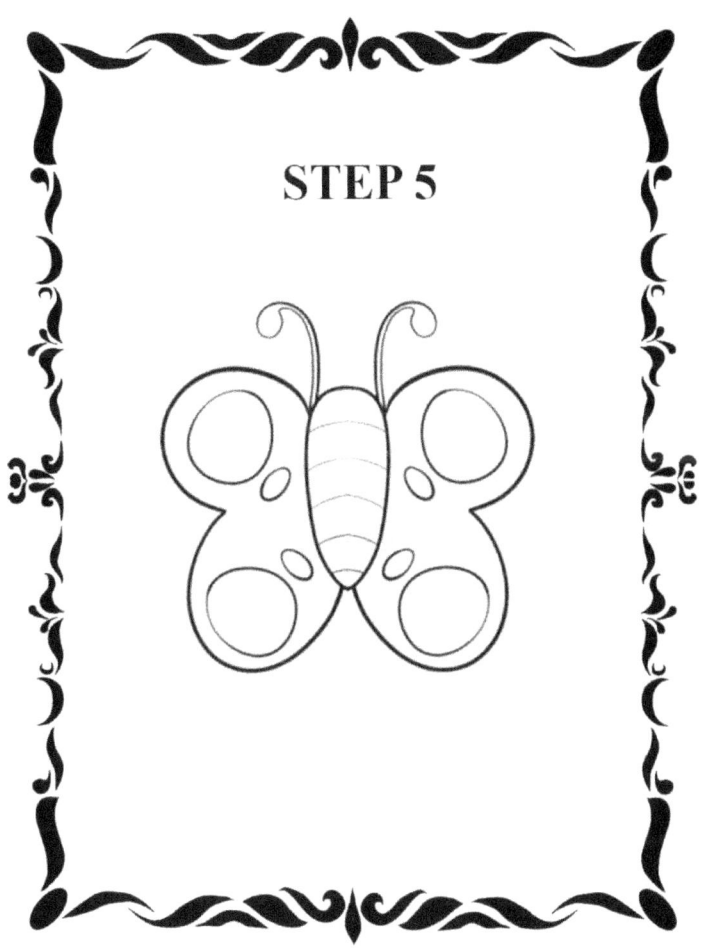

FLOWER
BUTTERFLY

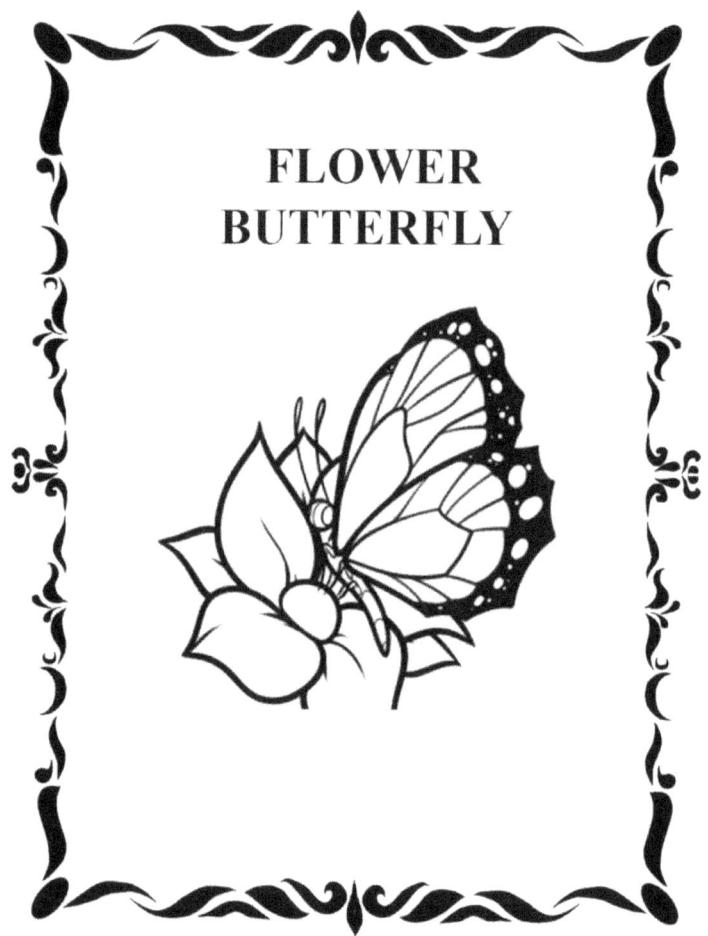

STEP 1

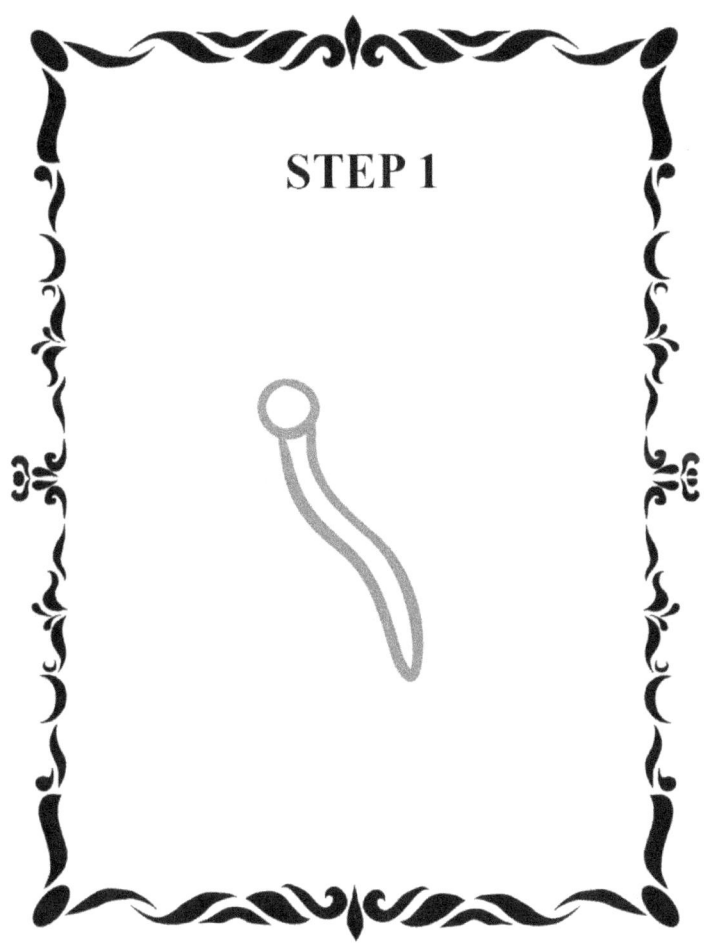

STEP 2

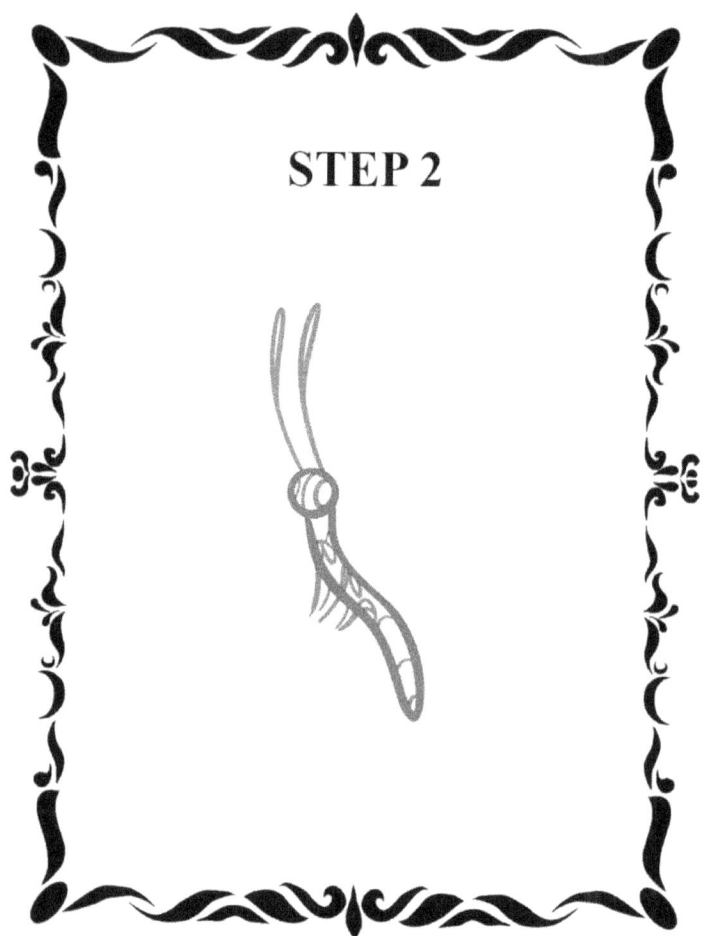

STEP 3

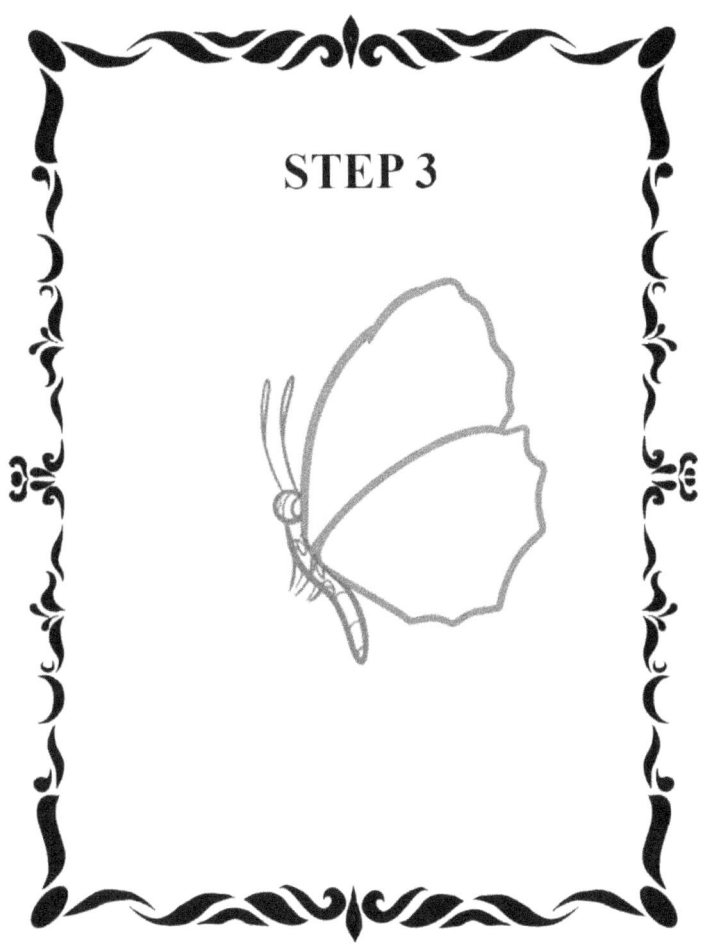

STEP 4

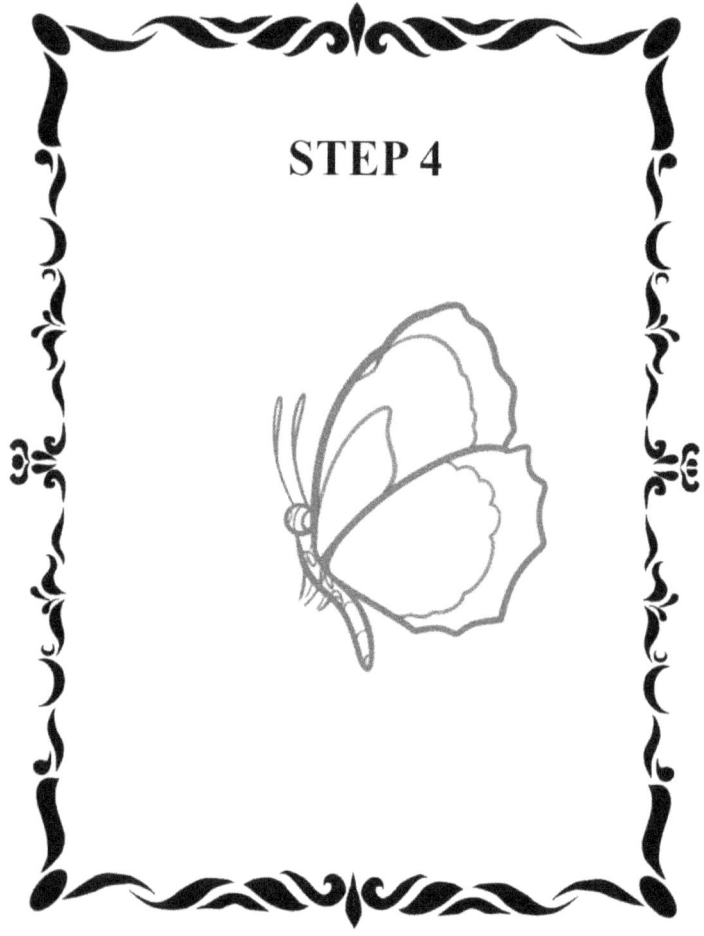

STEP 5

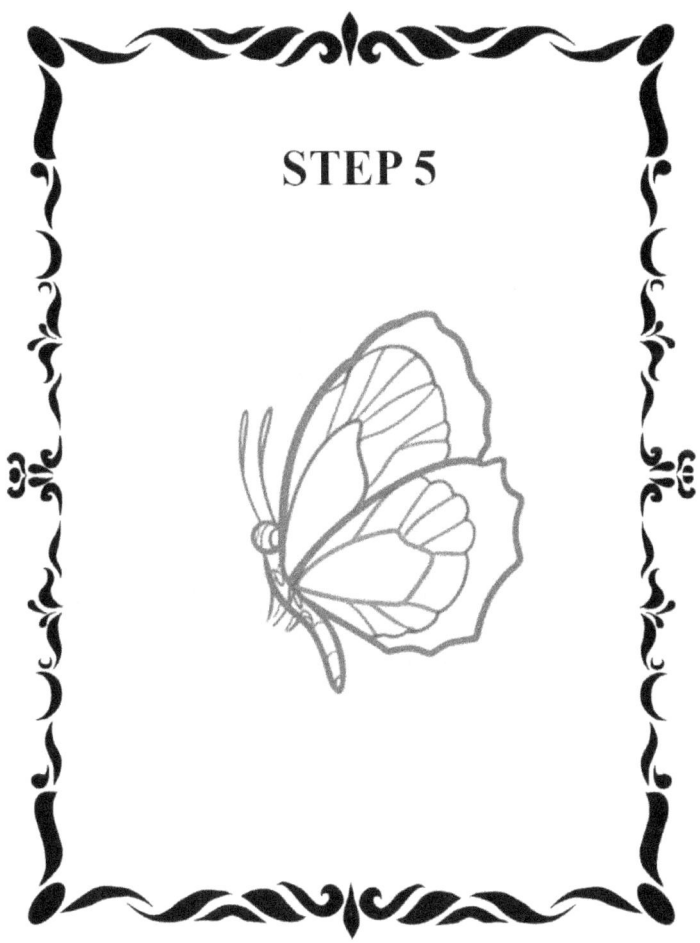

48

STEP 6

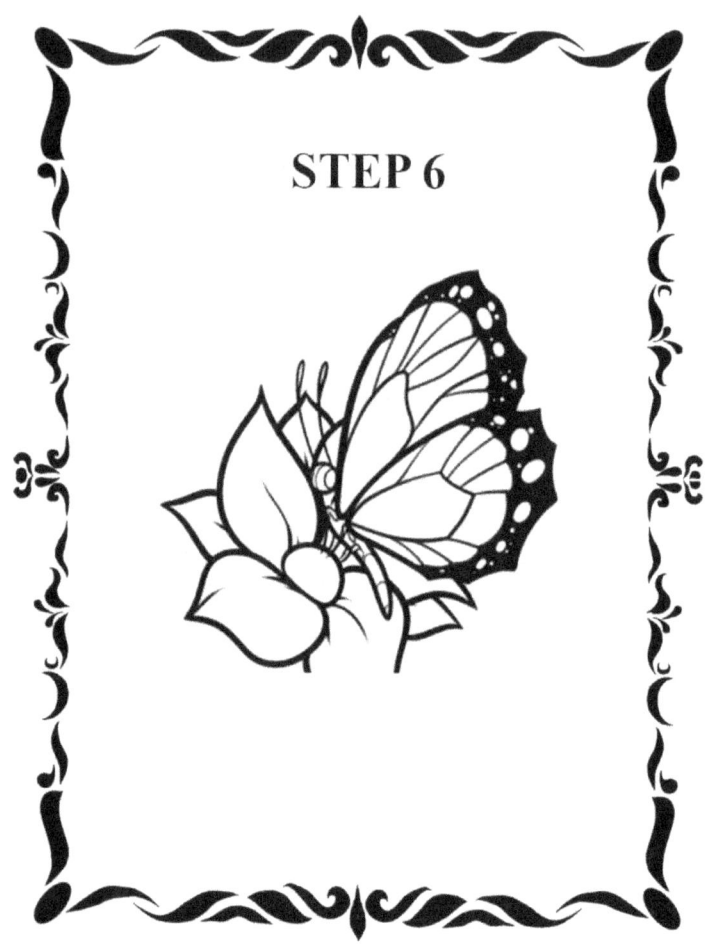

SIMPLE
BUTTERFLY

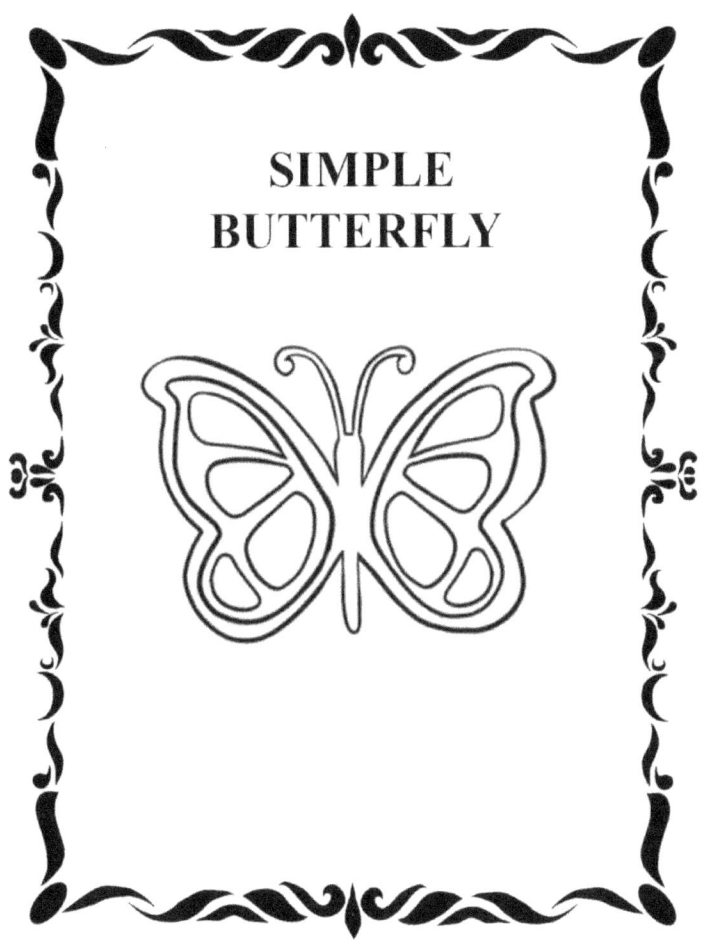

STEP 1

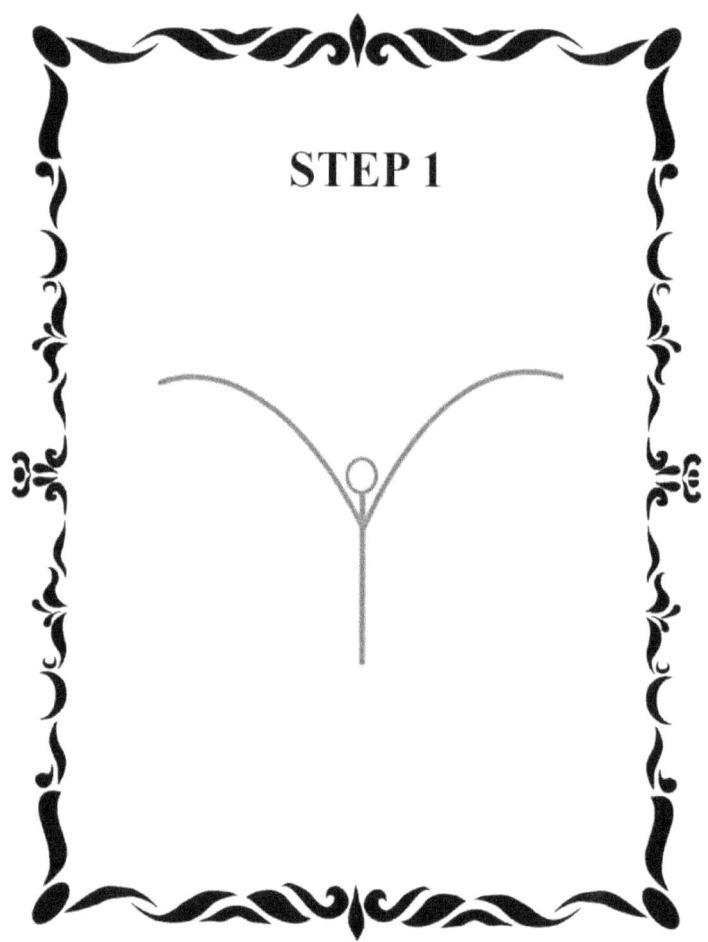

STEP 2

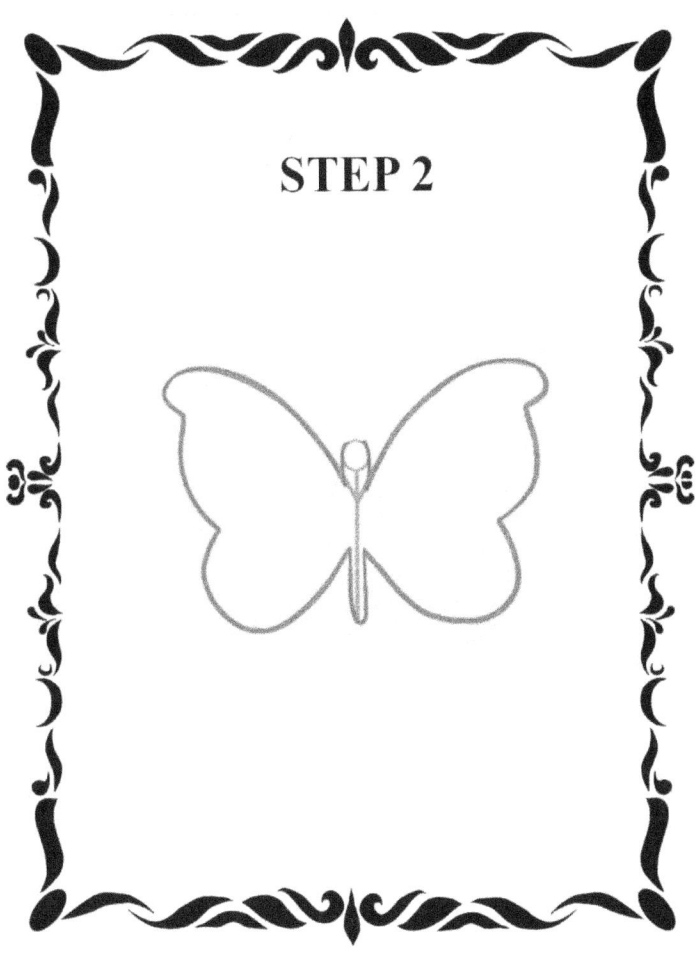

STEP 3

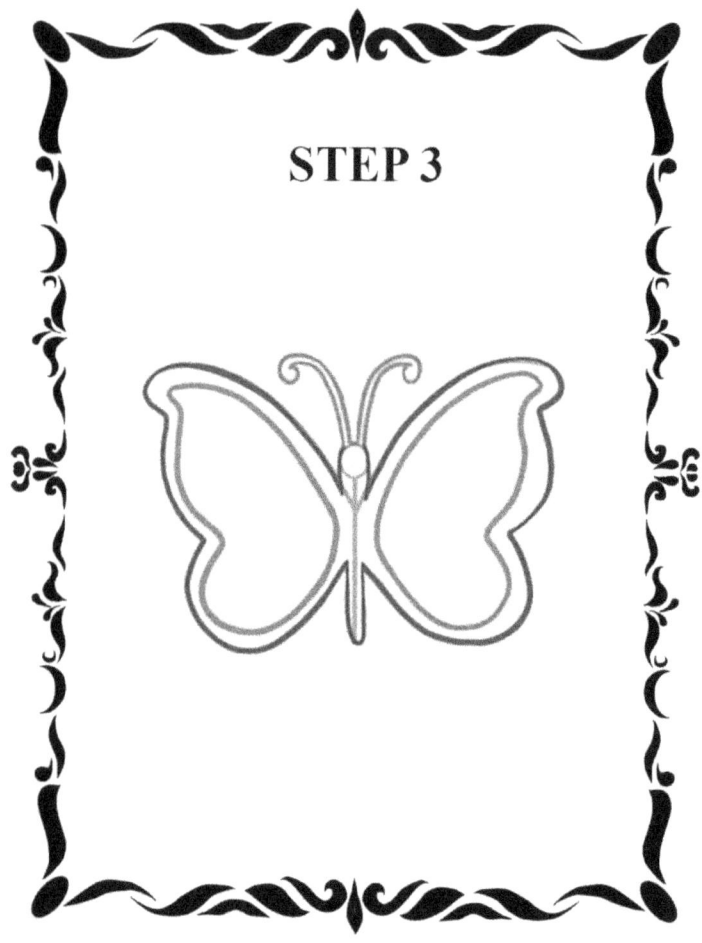

53

STEP 4

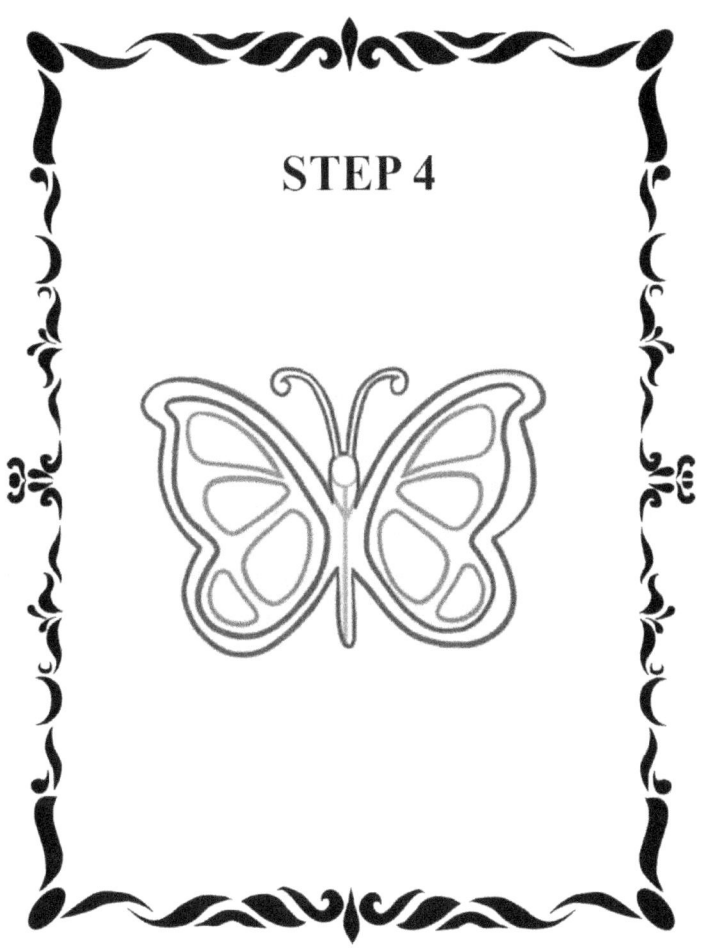

STEP 5

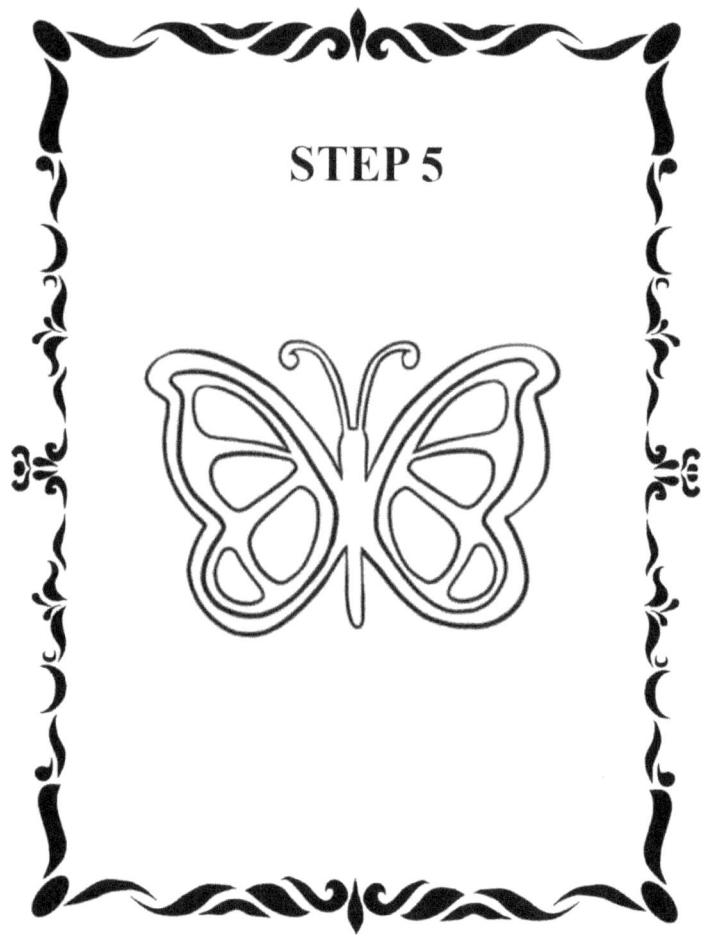

55

SKULL BUTTERFLY

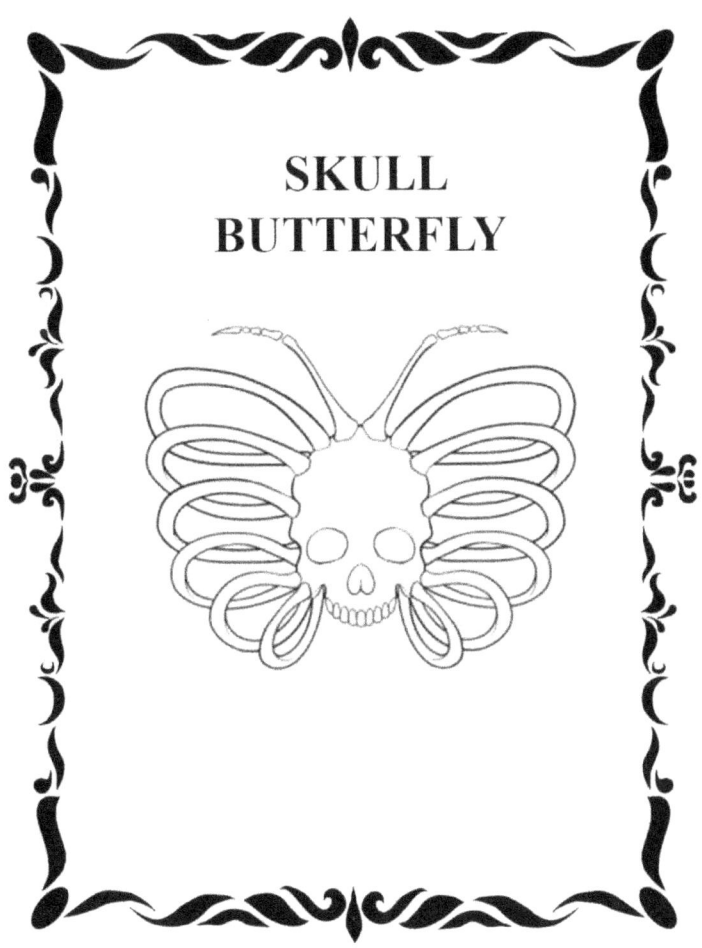

STEP 1

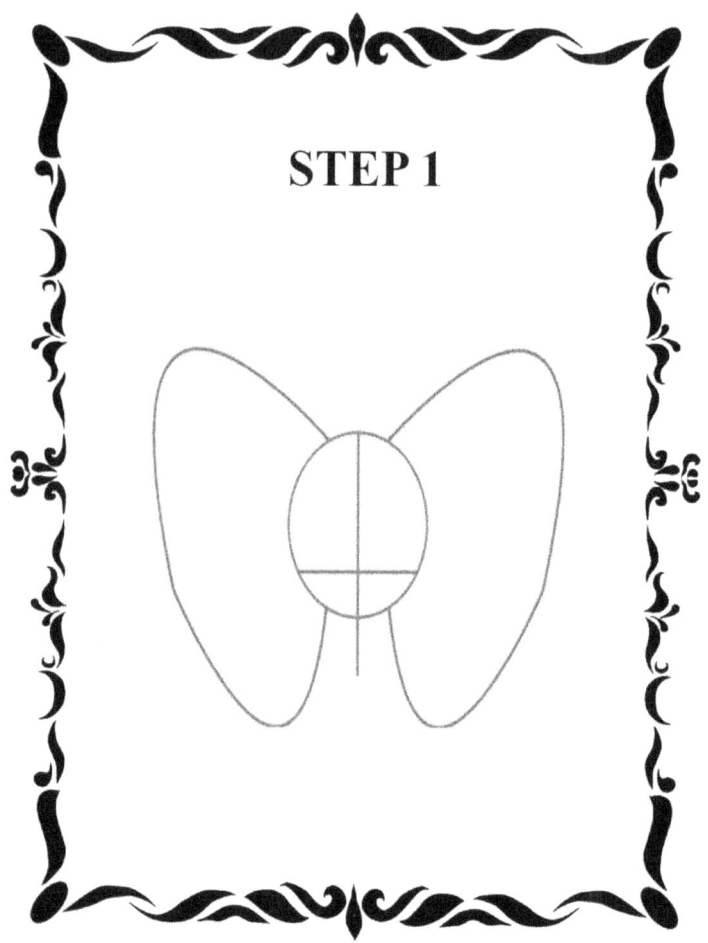

STEP 2

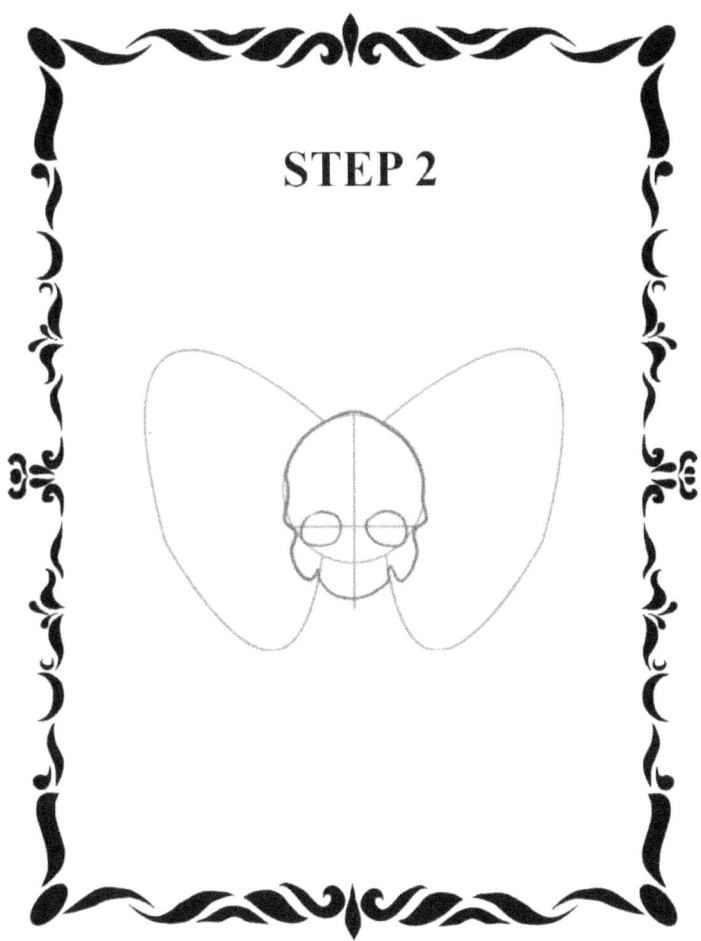

STEP 3

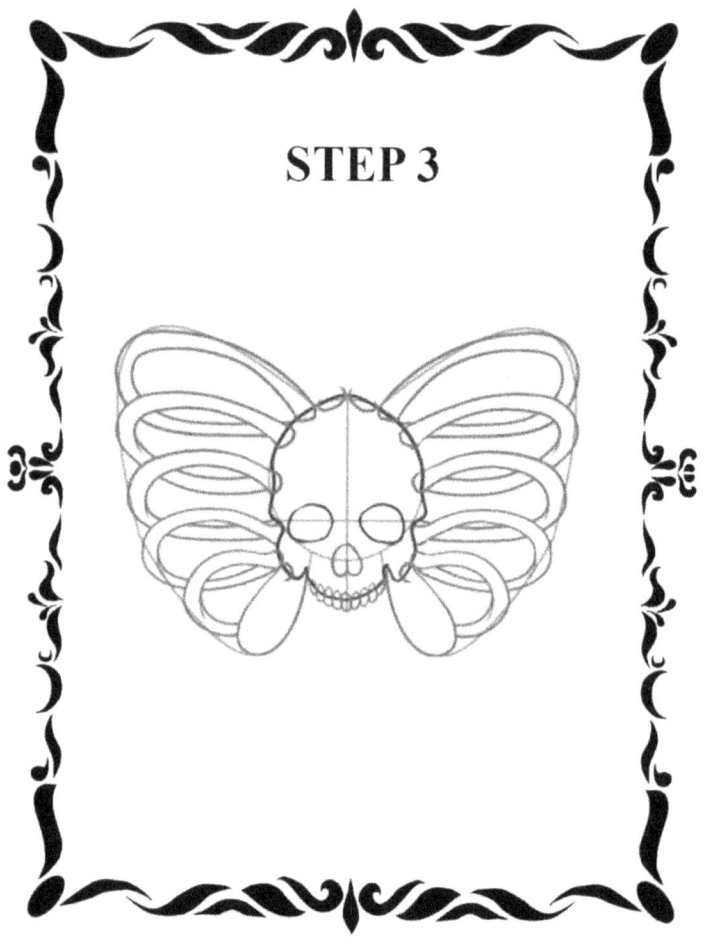

STEP 4

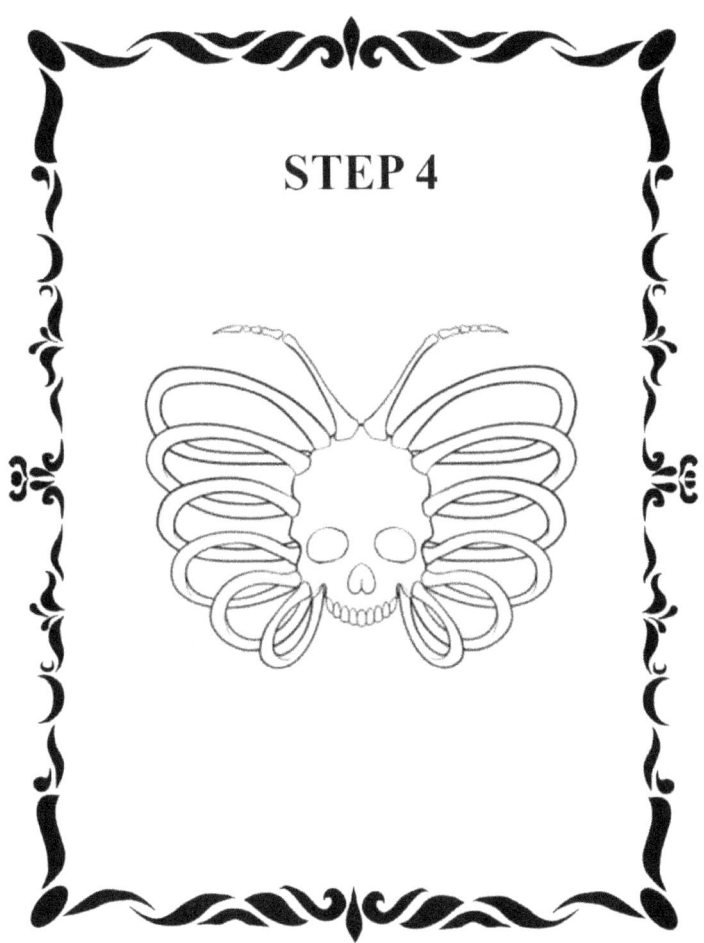

SPRING
BUTTERFLY

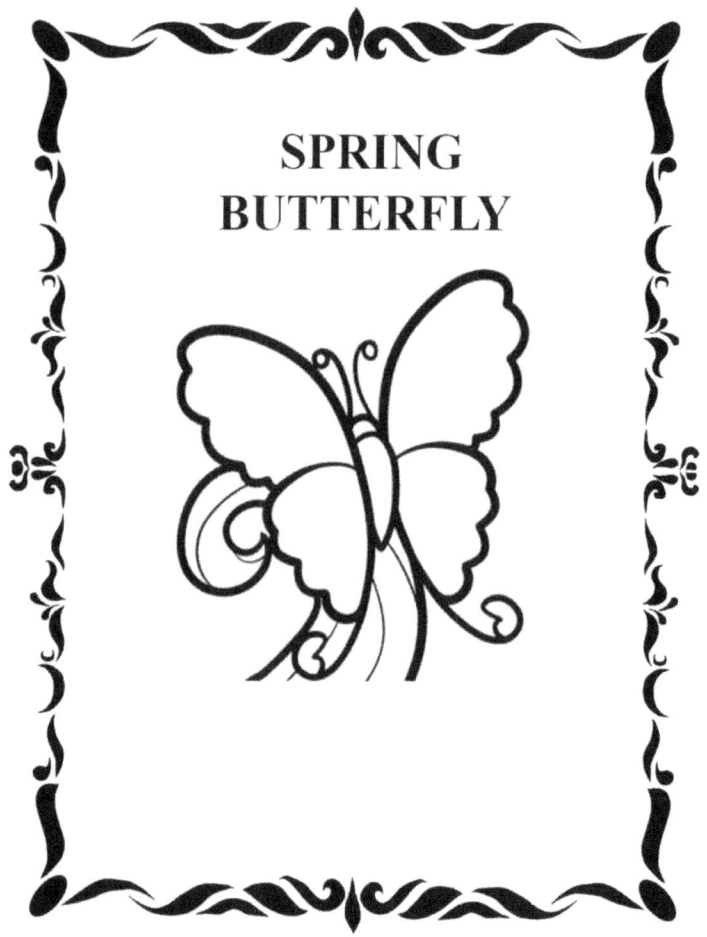

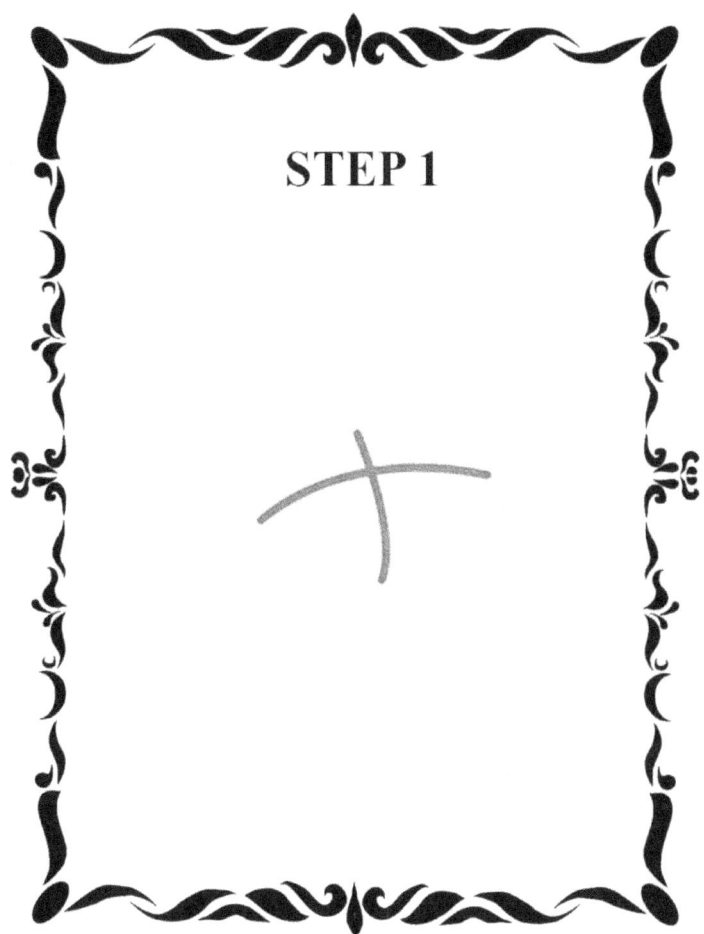

STEP 1

STEP 2

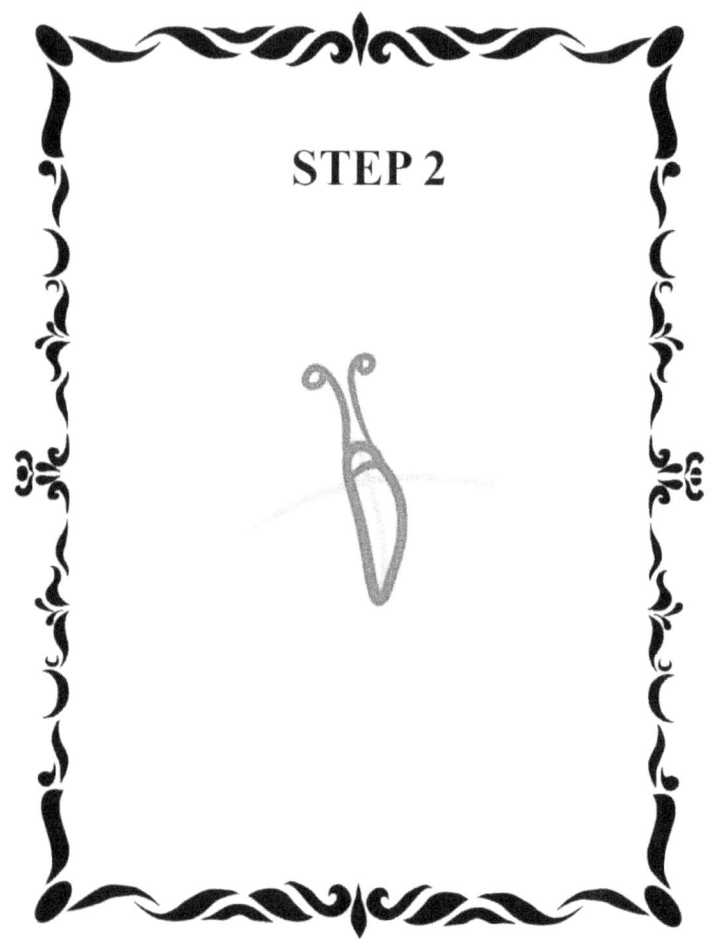

STEP 3

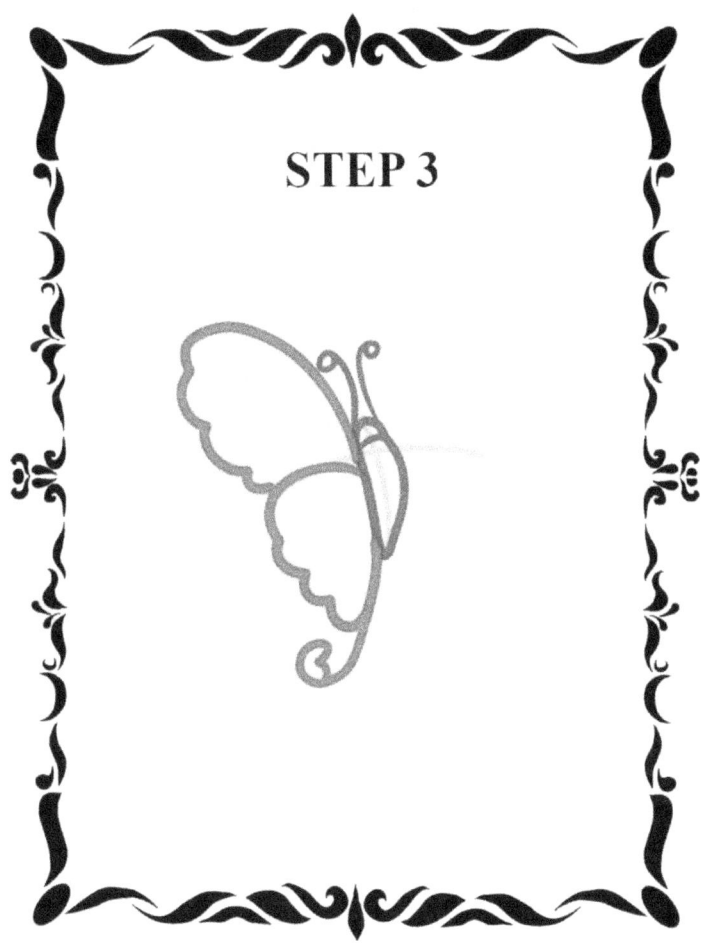

64

STEP 4

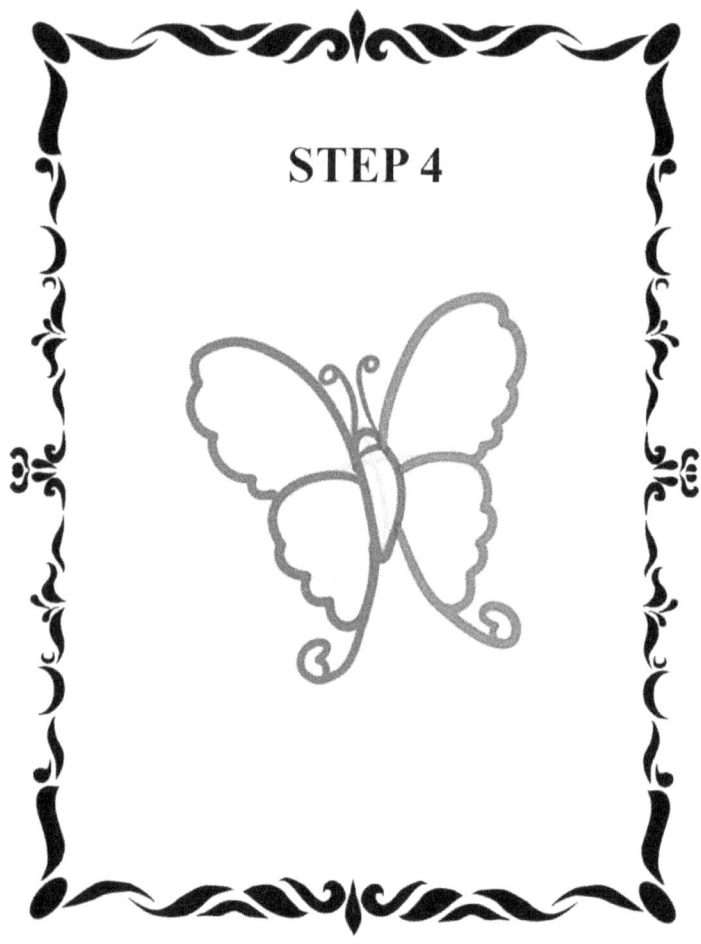

STEP 5

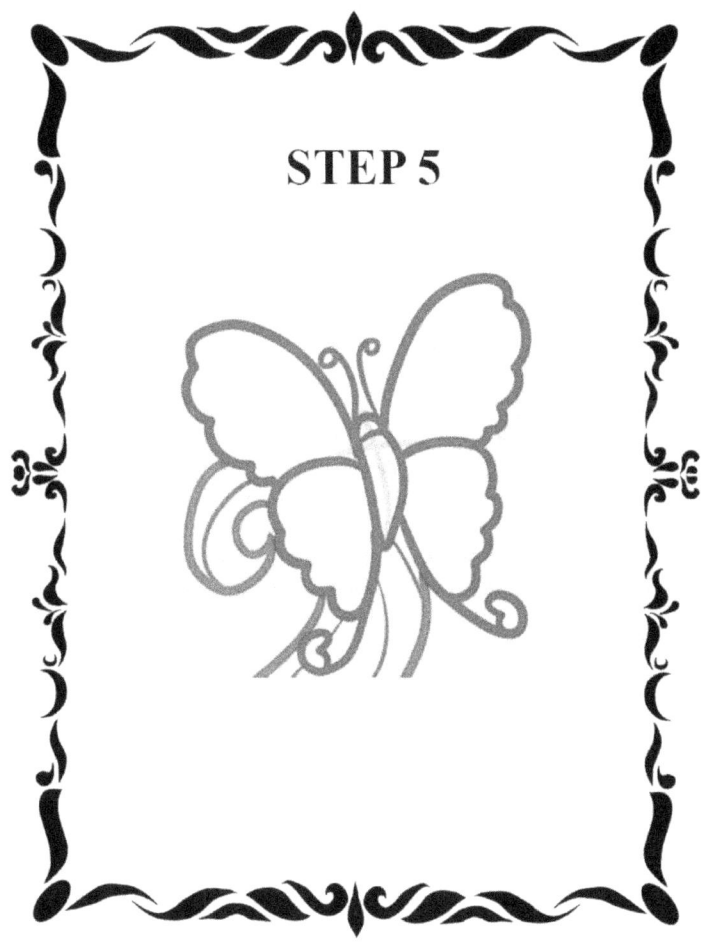

STEP 6

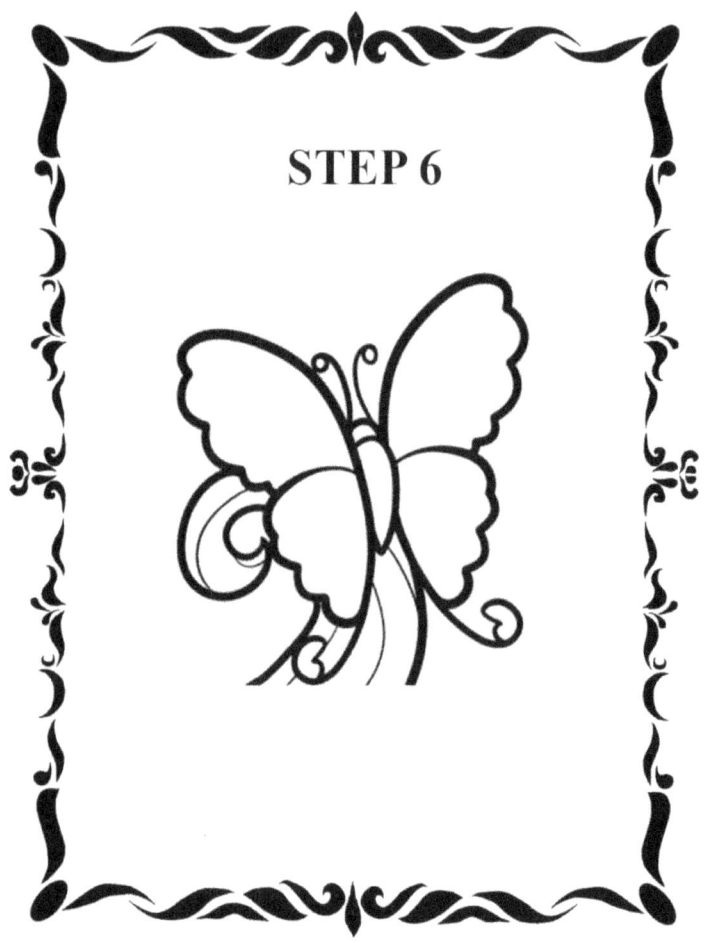

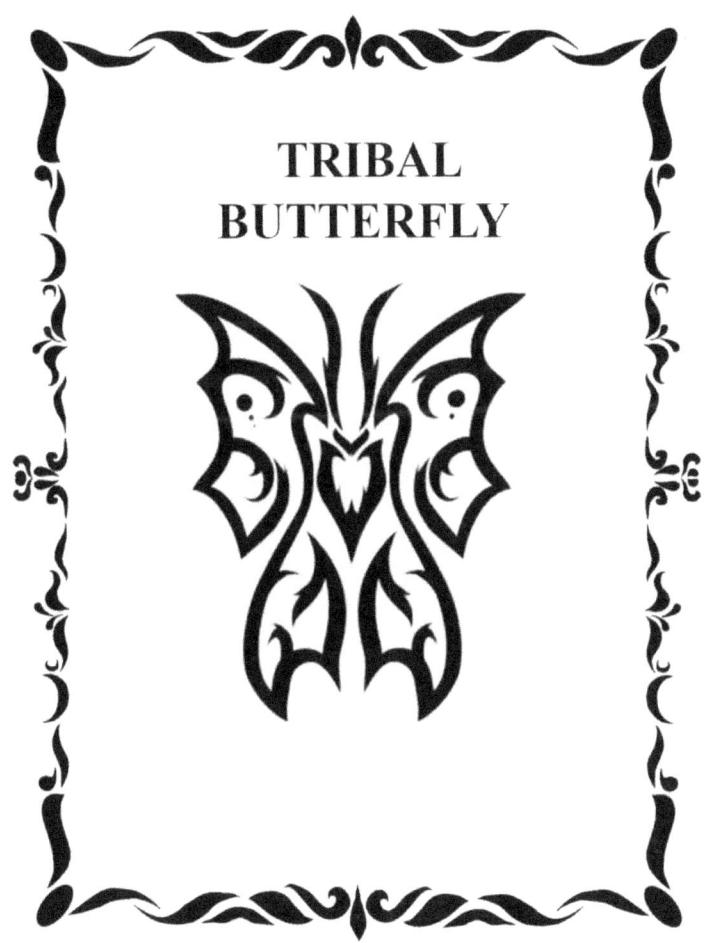

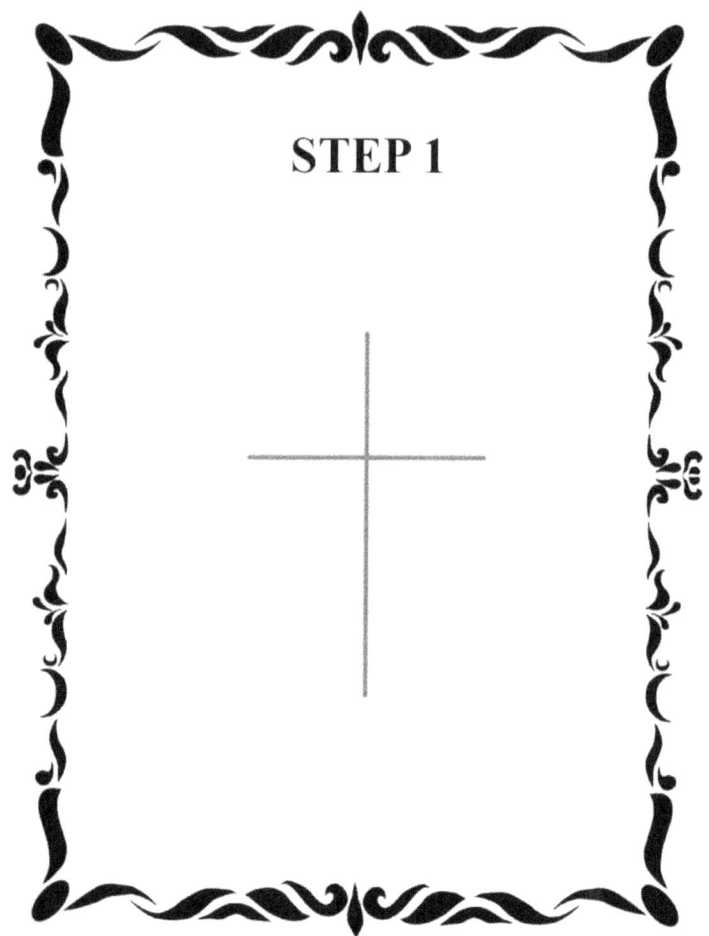

STEP 1

STEP 2

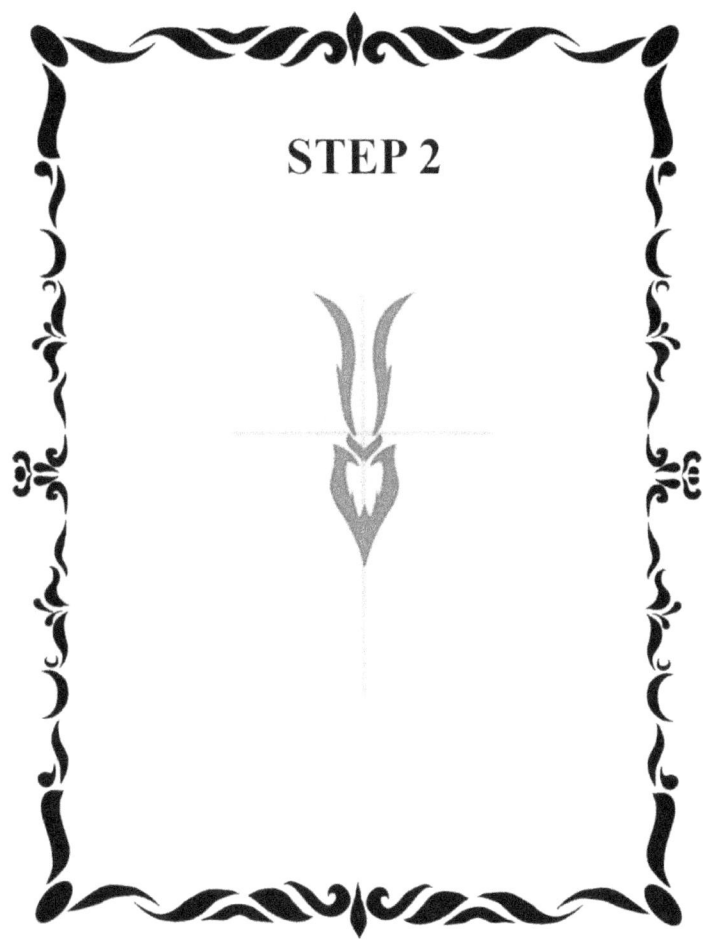

70

STEP 3

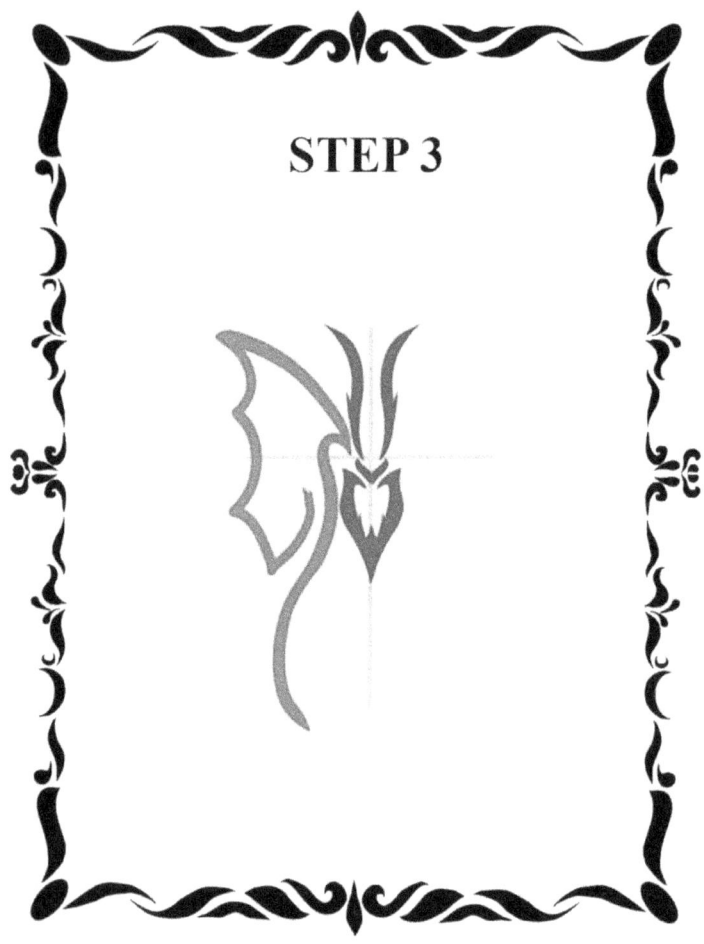

71

STEP 4

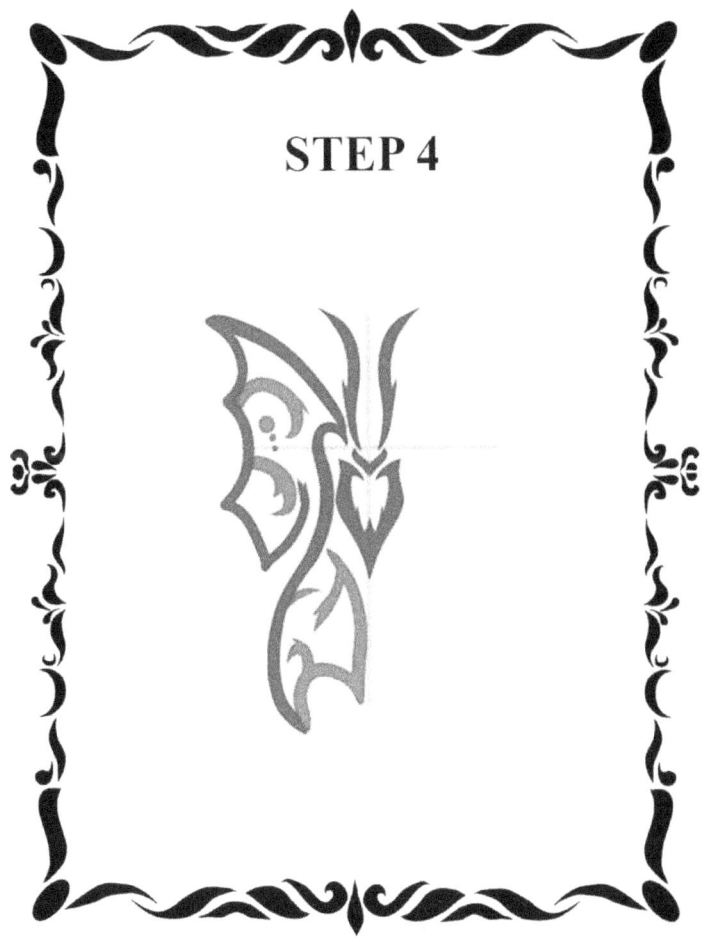

STEP 5

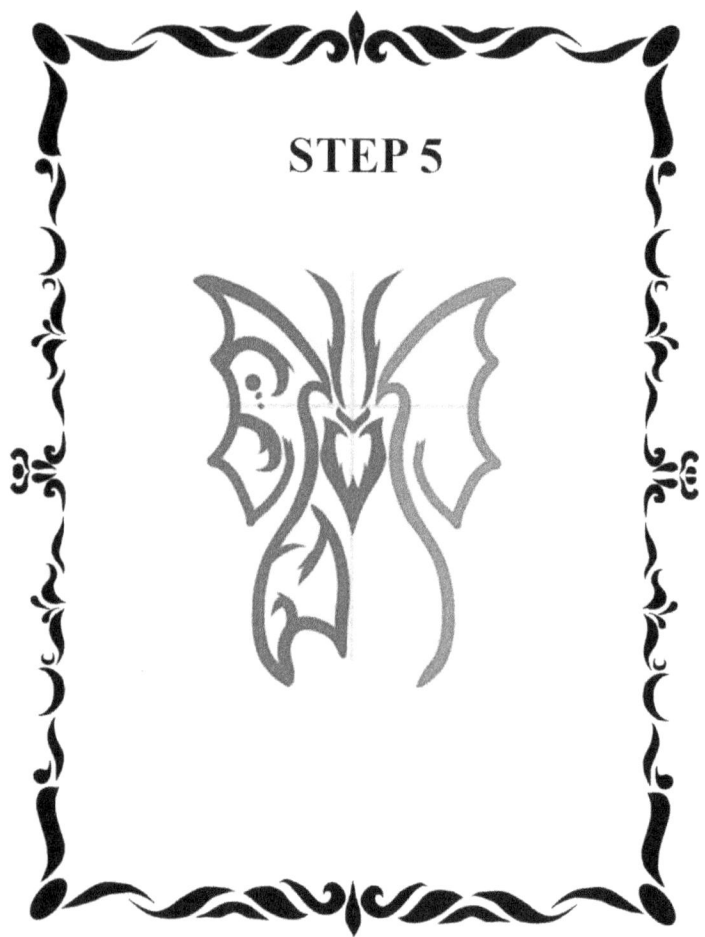

STEP 6

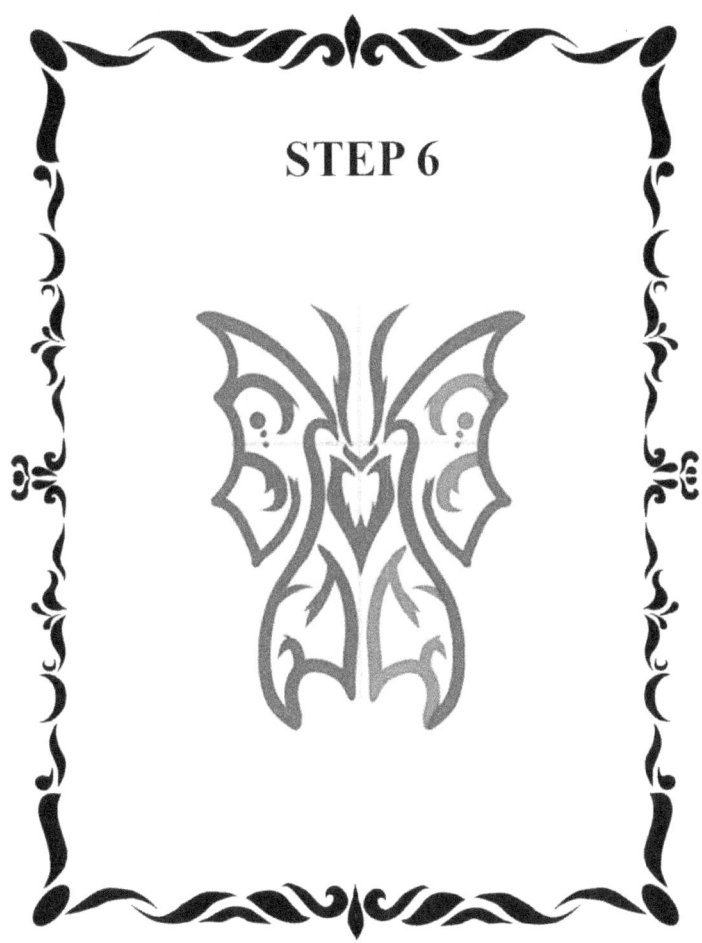

STEP 7

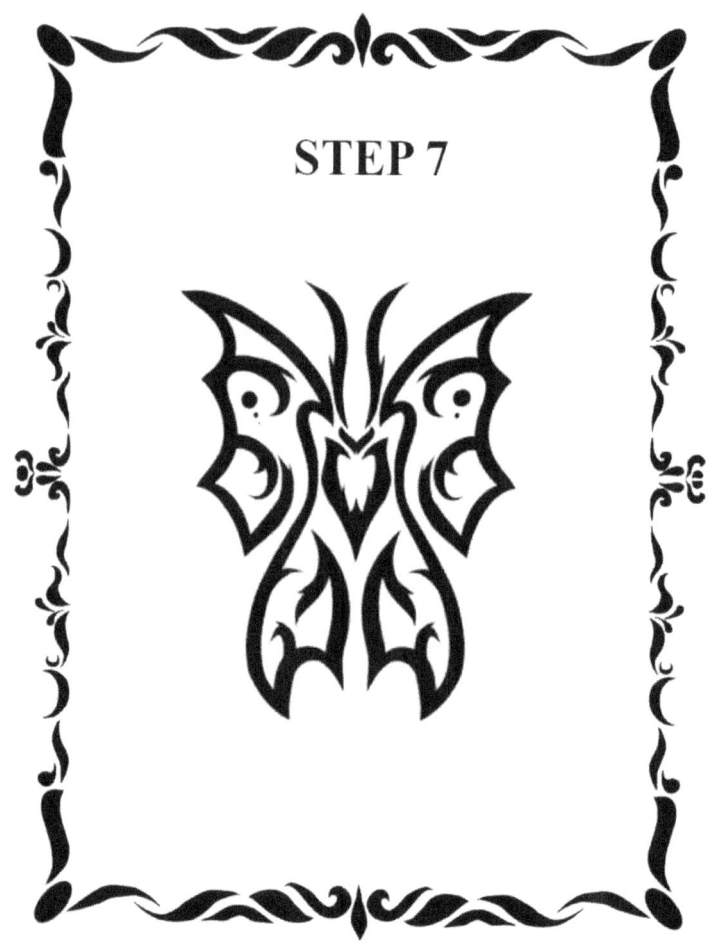

www.ingramcontent.com/pod-product-compliance
Lightning Source LLC
Chambersburg PA
CBHW071620170526
45166CB00003B/1132